THE TOP 11 OF EVERYTHING GERS...

Rangers

IT'S NOT TRIVIA, IT'S MORE IMPORTANT THAN THAT

ROUGH GUIDE
11s

Written by
Mark Benstead

Series editor
Paul Simpson

Text editors
Helen Rodiss, Michaela Bushell

Production
Ian Cranna, Tim Oldham, Tim
Harrison, Ann Oliver

Cover and book design
Sharon O'Connor

Cover image
Pascal Sacleux/Stock
Image/Alamy

Thanks to
Simon Kanter, Mark Ellingham,
Andrew Lockett, Emma
Koubayssi, Keith Jackson,
Robert McElroy
Special thanks to my mum for
all her help with everything,
and to Helene for her support
when I was starting out.

Printed in Spain
by Graphy Cems

This edition published
July 2005 was prepared by
Haymarket Customer
Publishing for
Rough Guides Ltd,
80 Strand, London, WC2R ORL

Distributed by the
Penguin Group
Penguin Books Ltd,
27 Wrights Lane,
London W8 5TZ

A catalogue record for this
book is available from the
British Library

ISBN 1-84353-564-5

Contents

ABSOLUTE BEST MOMENTS

11 of the happiest days in Rangers history

1. Rangers 3 Dynamo Moscow 2 Cup Winners' Cup, 24 May 1972
Four minutes into the second-half Rangers were 3-0 up and heading for an easy victory, but the Russians scored on the hour and got a second three minutes from time. In a nerve-racking finish, with fans invading the pitch, the Gers held out to lift their first and only European trophy.

2. Dundee United 0 Rangers 1 7 May 1997
Brian Laudrup met a Charlie Miller cross to score the only goal of the game sealing Rangers' ninth successive league championship.

3. Hibs 1 Rangers 1 29 March 1975
Ex-Hibee striker Colin Stein's goal secured a point for Rangers and the league title. This scuppered the Celtic's chances of recording a historic tenth consecutive title.

4. Rangers 3 Clyde 0 7 January 1899
Rangers become the first side to play a league season with a 100 per cent record.

5. The 1948/49 Treble season
The Gers bag their first Treble, defeating Raith Rovers 2-0 in the League Cup and Clyde 4-1 in the Scottish Cup. They win the league by a point over Dundee.

6. Rangers 7 Dundee 0 17 December 1898
Rangers secured their first outright league title in emphatic style. (They'd shared the first-ever league title with Dumbarton in 1891.)

7. Rangers 6 Dunfermline Athletic 1 25 April 2003
Heading into the final game of the season, Rangers and Celtic were level on points

with equal goal difference. The title would be decided by what happened in the season's final games, which took place simultaneously. Rangers were at home to Dunfermline, while Celtic were away at Kilmarnock. The Gers scored first through Michael Mols but Dair equalised for the Pars. Both Rangers and Celtic then scored in the 16th minute though Caniggia and Sutton, before Arveladze put Rangers 3-1 up. At this stage the title was heading to Ibrox. But just before half-time Sutton grabbed his second and then Alan Thompson scored from the spot shortly after the break to put the Hoops 3-0 up and in the driving seat. Ronald de Boer was next to score on 64 minutes and Stevie Thompson hit the net three minutes later to make it 5-1 and give Rangers the edge. Alan Thompson then blasted a second penalty over the bar but Stilian Petrov scored to pull them level on points and goal difference with just seven minutes to go. A play-off looked on the cards when Rangers were awarded a 90th-minute penalty. Mikel Arteta kept his cool to win the league for the Gers.

8. The 1992/93 season
Rangers won their fifth Treble. They finished nine points ahead of Aberdeen in the league, and beat their rivals from the north in both cup finals – after being drawn away in every round of the Scottish Cup. Walter Smith's team only narrowly missed out on European success that year, too. Undefeated in the Champions League, they went out due to a poorer head-to-head goals tally than eventual winners Marseille.

9. "Go on Gazza! Give us something!"
April 1996, Ibrox. Rangers are level 1-1 with Aberdeen with nine minutes to go. The Gers need to win to clinch the title. A team-mate shouts "Go on Gazza! Give us something" – more in desperation than hope. Gazza wins a 50/50 ball in his own half and starts to run like a demented spider. He beats two Dons at the start of his run and then, just as two defenders try to sandwich him, he fends them off, runs into the penalty area, evades a last lunging tackle and slides the ball home. 2-1 to Rangers and the title is won if it stays like that. But it doesn't. Gazza scores again – from the spot – for his hat-trick and to settle the issue.

10. Celtic 0 Rangers 1 League Cup final, 24 October 1970
A 16-year-old rises above the Hoops' defence to head home the only goal of the game. It won't be the last time Derek Johnstone features on a scoresheet.

11. Rangers 3 Celtic 0 Scottish Cup final replay, 16 May 1963
Widely seen as one of Rangers' most exciting performances. Ralph Brand scored twice to add to one from Davie Wilson as the Light Blues ran riot. Had they not eased off as the match went on, it could have been even more embarrassing for the Hoops. There was hardly a Celtic fan left in Hampden when the third goal went in.

ALMOST A GER

11 international stars who could have become Teddy Bears

1. Gianluca Vialli
The Italian striker is quoted as saying:"If Ruud (Gullit) hadn't wanted me, I'd have gone to Rangers."The Dutchman's approach saw the millionaire head to the King's Road of Chelsea rather than the Copland Road of Ibrox.

2. Craig Bellamy
After the Newcastle striker joined Celtic on loan in 2005, Rangers manager Alex McLeish admitted that Rangers, too, had enquired about the striker.

3. Teemu Tiano
The up-and-coming Finnish play-maker was in talks with Rangers in early 2005 but opted to sign a pre-contract with Tottenham.

4. John Hartson
The Welshman almost completed a move to Ibrox in August 2000 but it collapsed at the eleventh hour after he failed a medical. He may have been disappointed, but did he really have to join Celtic?

5. Florin Raducioiu
The Gers tried to take the Romanian striker from Español in the mid-1990s but eventually missed out. Given his later performances for West Ham, fans could be forgiven for thinking this was a narrow escape. However, it's worth remembering that the club bought Oleg 'five goals in a World Cup match' Salenko instead. The Russian hardly set the heather alight in his time in Glasgow.

6. Karl-Heinz Riedle
The German striker and European Cup winner was close to a £2m move to Ibrox in 1996. In the end Borussia Dortmund offered him an improved deal to stay at the Westfalenstadion. Riedle eventually joined Liverpool.

> AS THE LIGHT BLUES RAN RIOT, THERE WAS HARDLY A CELTIC FAN LEFT IN HAMPDEN – 1963 CUP FINAL REPLAY

7. Emmanuel Petit
The French World Cup winner was close to a move to Ibrox before he eventually joined Arsenal in 1997. The Gers were one of four clubs in the race to sign the midfielder, offering £4m for his services. However Manu was eventually won over by his former manager Arsène Wenger.

8. Robbie Fowler
Rangers were linked with a move for the striker on more than one occasion, the most notable being in January 1999. The forward was in a contract dispute with Liverpool and the Gers were understood to be ready to offer £10m for him.

9. Paul Ince
Impressed by Gazza's tales of life at Ibrox, the England midfielder came close to a move to Glasgow in 2002.

10. Mario Jardel
The Brazilian striker was on the verge of joining Rangers in 1995/96 from Gremio but the move failed to materialise and he went to Porto instead. He was again linked with a switch to Ibrox in 2003, but judging by his waddling performances for Bolton shortly afterwards, most Gers fans will probably be glad he didn't.

11. Stephane Henchoz
After falling out of favour at Anfield in 2004, the defender was offered a contract by Rangers. Although interested in a move to Ibrox, the Swiss star wanted a longer contract than the six-month initial deal the Gers had offered. As time drew on, Celtic showed an interest and he completed a free transfer to Parkhead in January 2005.

AT THE MOVIES
The current 11's favourite films

1. **Michael Ball** *The Shawshank Redemption*
2. **Thomas Buffel** *Gladiator*
3. **Dragan Mladenovich** *Forrest Gump*
4. **Bob Malcolm** *The Shawshank Redemption*
5. **Marvin Andrews** *The Godfather*
6. **Dado Prso** *Gladiator*
7. **Alan Hutton** *Troy*
8. **Chris Burke** *Finding Nemo*
9. **Steven Thompson** *Star Wars*
10. **Gregory Vignal** *Bad Boys*
11. **Barry Ferguson** *Trainspotting*

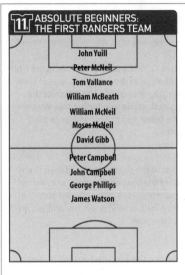

ABSOLUTE BEGINNERS: THE FIRST RANGERS TEAM

John Yuill
Peter McNeil
Tom Vallance
William McBeath
William McNeil
Moses McNeil
David Gibb
Peter Campbell
John Campbell
George Phillips
James Watson

The first Rangers team to play a competitive match, v Oxford (Scottish Cup), Fleshers' Haugh, 10 October 1874. Rangers won 2-0.

ATTILA STRIKES AGAIN

11 great Mark Hateley moments

1. Rangers 2 Aberdeen 0 11 May 1991
Rangers needed to beat Aberdeen at Ibrox to win the Premier Division ahead of the Dons. Attila scored twice to ensure the title went to Glasgow. His first came as he rose above present Gers boss Alex McLeish to head home from Mark Walters's cross. His second came as he followed up Mo Johnston's saved effort.

2. Leeds United 1 Rangers 2 European Cup, 4 November 1992
A spectacular 25-yard shot on the turn looped over John Lukic in the Leeds goal. It was a breathtaking strike by Hateley and silenced the Elland Road crowd.

3. Rangers 2 Marseille 2 Champions League, 25 November 1992
Hateley dived to head home inches off the ground as Rangers came from behind to draw 2-2 with Marseille in Glasgow.

4. Aberdeen 0 Rangers 1 2 February 1993
A classic Hateley goal handed the Gers a vital Premier Division win at Pittodrie.

Gary Stevens crossed from the right and Hateley rose above the Dons' defenders to hammer a header into the net.

5. Celtic 0 Rangers 1 16 March 1997
Hateley had moved south to join Ray Wilkins at QPR, but answered an SOS call from the Gers to return to Ibrox. Rangers had crashed out of the Scottish Cup and were without any fit strikers heading into the all-important last Old Firm clash of the season. A win for Celtic would see the Hoops back in the race for the title. Walter Smith called up Hateley three days before the game and the big striker proved crucial in setting up the only goal of the game.

6. Celtic 1 Rangers 3 30 October 1994
The Gers were looking to atone for a poor start to the season that had seen them crash out of Europe at the first hurdle, go out of the League Cup to Falkirk and fall behind Celtic in the league. Hateley led by example, scoring the opener from the edge of the box before adding a second just on half-time. The win maintained an unbeaten run that continued until the end of the year.

7. The 1993/94 season
Hateley became the first Englishman to be named the Scottish Football Writers' Player of the Year.

8. Rangers 2 Airdrie 1 Scottish Cup final, 9 May 1992
Hateley and McCoist underlined the threat of their strike partnership by grabbing a goal apiece as the Gers lifted the Cup and, in the process, their 12th Double.

9. Rangers 2 Aberdeen 1 Scottish Cup final, 29 May 1993
Hateley scored in the Scottish Cup final for the second year in a row as Rangers again ran out 2-1 winners in a thrilling encounter with Aberdeen.

10. Rangers 3 Levski Sofia 2 Champions League, 15 September 1993
Hateley was both hero and villain in this match. The striker scored two trademark headers but was at fault for a Levski goal as the Gers won 3-2.

11. Rangers 2 Aberdeen 1 25 October 1992
The game came just days after a gruelling Battle of Britain clash with Leeds United at Ibrox in the European Cup. With the game poised at 1-1, pressure from Hateley forced the Dons' Gary Smith to put the ball into his own net. The move gave the Gers victory and the first of what would be a triple haul of trophies.

THE AULD ENEMY

11 Englishmen who played for the Gers

1. Terry Butcher

Formed a dominating defensive partnership with Richard Gough after his move from Ipswich Town in 1986. Butcher was a tremendous leader on the pitch and an ambassador for the club off it. After leaving Ibrox he had less-than-successful spells in management with Coventry and Sunderland, but he is now firmly climbing the managerial ladder as boss of Motherwell. After taking over the Lanarkshire outfit he has guided them away from relegation, through administration and into their first cup final in over a decade. A potential manager for Rangers?

2. Mark Hateley

Joined Rangers in 1990 via Coventry, Portsmouth, AC Milan and Monaco. He had a difficult start to his time at Ibrox. Many fans saw him as a replacement for their favourite Ally McCoist and he was made to work for their respect. Ironically, Hateley eventually formed a hugely effective strike partnership with McCoist.

3. Trevor Steven

Joined the club from Everton for a tribunal-decided fee of £1.7m in 1989 and left for a brief spell with Marseille in 1991 before returning to Glasgow. Well-respected by staff and supporters, he made 184 appearances for the club.

4. Ray Wilkins

The Crab had already plied his trade with Manchester United and AC Milan before joining Rangers from Monaco in 1987. Family pressures meant he had to return to London after two years in Glasgow, but he became so popular with the fans that a packed Ibrox gave him a standing ovation after he finished his last game for the club.

5. Graham Roberts

The tough tackling defender played 69 times for the club before a massive bust-up with boss Graeme Souness after a 1-0 defeat by Aberdeen saw him sold to Chelsea.

6. Paul Gascoigne

If Gazza's spell at Ibrox were a Clint Eastwood movie, it would be *The Good, The Bad And The Ugly*. For a while, the Gers got the best of Gazza, possibly because, Terry Butcher says, "He was physically scared of Archie Knox, who sometimes resorted to extreme measures to get his point across." But the bad – reckless performances in Europe – and the ugly – flute-playing in the derby, his appearance in a bar in New York in Celtic gear – were such that Walter Smith felt obliged to sell him.

7. Nigel Spackman

Arrived at Ibrox from QPR as Ray Wilkins moved in the opposite direction. Shortly after his arrival he scored the winner against Celtic on New Year's Day. He won three championships with the Gers to add to one in England with Liverpool.

8. Michael Ball

Joined the Gers from his boyhood team Everton for £6.5m. The defender hasn't enjoyed the best of luck since his move to Ibrox – injury kept him on the sidelines from December 2001 to August 2003. When he eventually returned to action there was more frustration: a clause in his contract stated that when he had played 65 games for the Gers, a further £500,000 would be paid to Everton. The cash-strapped club wasn't keen to cough up, so the defender was used sparingly to avoid triggering the payment. Eventually the two clubs came to an agreement and Ball was finally able to work on establishing himself in the Rangers team.

9. Chris Woods

The signing of the England international was a signal of intent by the Rangers board that they intended to compete with the best. In his first season, Woods helped the club to win the league championship – he would win three more with the Gers.

10. Mark Walters

When the speedy winger joined the club from Aston Villa in 1987 he became the first black player to play for the club in more than 50 years.

11. Terry Hurlock

Joined from Millwall and was renowned for a tough-tackling style that often brought bookings. Only lasted one season at Ibrox before moving to Southampton.

AUTOBIOGRAPHIES

The story of my life, by 11 Rangers players

1. *L.A. Confidential*, Lorenzo Amoruso
2. *A Captain's Story*, John Greig
3. *Both Sides of the Border*, Terry Butcher
4. *Captain of Scotland*, George Young
5. *Field of Dreams, My Ibrox Years*, Richard Gough
6. *A Football Revolutionary*, Graeme Souness
7. *Home and Away*, Mark Hateley

8. *Mo – The Maurice Johnston Story*, Mo Johnston
9. *Scotland's For Me*, Andy Goram
10. *Ha Way the Lad*, Paul Gascoigne
11. *Rangers: My Team*, Derek Johnstone

BAD DAYS FOR THE BANK MANAGER

11 biggest transfer fees paid by Rangers

1. Tore Andre Flo from Chelsea, £12.5m
2. Michael Ball from Everton, £6.5m
3. Mikel Arteta from Barcelona, £5.8m
4. Andrei Kanchelskis from Fiorentina, £5.5m
5. Arthur Numan from PSV, £5m
6. Giovanni van Bronckhorst from Feyenoord, £5m
7. Ronald de Boer from Barcelona, £4.5m
8. Barry Ferguson from Blackburn Rovers, £4.5m
9. Paul Gascoigne from Lazio
   Bert Konterman Feyenoord, £4.3m each
10. **Gabriel Amato** from Mallorca, £4.2m
11. Michael Mols from FC Utrecht
   Colin Hendry Blackburn Rovers,
   Jorg Albertz from SV Hamburg, £4m each

BALANCING THE BOOKS

Rangers' 11 most lucrative sales

1. Giovanni van Bronckhorst to Arsenal, £8.5m
2. Jean-Alain Boumsong to Newcastle United, £8m
3. Tore Andre Flo to Sunderland, £6.75m

4. **Barry Ferguson** to Blackburn Rovers, £6.5m
5. **Trevor Steven** to Olympique Marseille, £5m
6. **Claudio Reyna** to Sunderland, £4.75m
7. **Duncan Ferguson** to Everton, £3.75m
   Gabriel Amato to Cremio, £3.75m
9. **Paul Gascoigne** to Middlesbrough, £3.5m
10. **Stephane Guivarc'h** to Auxerre, £3.4m
11. **Jonatan Johansson** to Charlton Athletic, £3.25m

BEARS WITH SORE HEADS

Not all publicity is good publicity

1. Andy Goram

'The Goalie' quits the Scotland squad ahead of France 1998. The keeper was almost certain to start as No 1, but pulled out after tabloid allegations over his private life. *The Sun* alleged he had paid ex-Celtic sales executive Janice Dunn £900 to have an abortion. He feared the paper would name his girlfriend at the time, Miriam Wylie.

2. Andy Goram (again)

After picking up a knee injury in 1994, Andy Goram was told to go on holiday to recuperate, in the hope he would heal in time for the Scottish Cup final. Goram went to Tenerife but there bumped into his former Oldham team-mates. Cue 'The Goalie' being coaxed into switching sun-loungers for sangria on the last two days of his holiday. He was due to fly home at 5am with his family but after one drink too many awoke at one – the next afternoon. He was trapped without clothes, money, his passport or, quite importantly, his family. After managing to organise a flight home through a friend back in Scotland and borrowing money and clothes, you would have thought Goram would sit tight and wait for his flight. Think again. He was soon out on the lash again, this time having to dodge reporters who'd heard he'd gone off the rails. He eventually made it home but the adventure almost ended his Ibrox career. He was slapped on the transfer list by Walter Smith but eventually escaped sale after proving his fitness through the following pre-season.

3. Fernando Ricksen

In November 2002, while entertaining friends, Fernando Ricksen got carried away. After a few drinks he decided to set off fireworks, even though it was 5am. His neighbour, Mr Killen, asked the Rangers star to curb his impromptu display but the Dutchman wasn't keen to comply. An angry exchange followed which saw Ricksen push his neighbour in the face and tell him to keep his nose out or else. Ricksen followed this by saying: "I know where you live." This might have sounded impressive in a gangster flick but didn't have the same impact in Newton Mearns, as Mr Killen of course lived next door. A year later Ricksen was fined £7,000 for setting off the fireworks.

4. Fernando Ricksen (again)

Just two days after being hit with a fine for his fireworks display Ricksen was again on the front pages, this time after spending the night with glamour model Jordan. The pair had whiled away the evening being entertained by a Hungarian lap-dancer named Carmen, before heading home for a spot of late-night trampolining.

> **IN HIS DRUNKEN STATE, McCALL THOUGHT IT WOULD BE CLEVER TO RIDE A MOTORBIKE THROUGH RECEPTION**

5. Fernando Ricksen (one more time)

In 2003 the Rangers team were in Greece ahead of a game against Panathinaikos when Ricksen thought it would be funny to push a middle-aged hotel guest into the pool. Unfortunately, the man in question was the Gers chairman, John McClelland, whose designer suit, mobile phone, digital camera and Cartier watch were ruined.

6. Stuart McCall

During their nine-in-a-row quest, the Rangers team were staying at a hotel when Stuart McCall is understood to have had one too many. In his drunken state the midfielder thought it would be clever to ride a motorbike through reception.

7. Paul Gascoigne

The allegations – and his admission – of spousal abuse finally soured Gazza's Rangers career. Sent off against Ajax the day before the story hit the tabloids, for some – notably Roddy Forsyth – he was never the same player again for the club. At this point, Walter Smith realised that Gazza would never be off the front pages.

8. Davie Robertson

Robertson wasn't generally a party animal. The defender's better half was rumoured to keep him on a tight leash, meaning he very rarely joined in with his team-mates' infamous drinking sessions. On the odd occasion he did, however, he more than made up for his absences. On one particular night he had more than his fair share to drink and found himself the worse for wear in Glasgow's Princess Square. The police arrived to find the left-back walking across the tops of parked cars. A night in jail followed and the story goes that his shoes were taken as evidence. That meant he had to stand outside the cells in his socks to wait for his less-than-impressed wife to collect him.

9. Mo Johnston

During the 1990/91 season Rangers were training in Italy. After a particularly heavy night's partying, Johnston came back to his room in a pretty bad way. The striker was sharing with Scott Nisbet who, unbeknown to Johnston, had dragged the mattress on to the floor as the bed wasn't long enough for him. Mo came crashing into the room and launched himself at the now mattress-less bed. The result wasn't pretty as the striker's face bounced off the uncovered bed frame. When the team flew home Johnston's battered and bruised face adorned the papers. This kind of publicity didn't help his Ibrox career. He was sold to Everton in November 1991.

> "NOT FOR ME WHISKY OR VODKA. I ALMOST GOT ADDICTED TO BAILEYS." LORENZO AMORUSO TELLS ALL

10. Barry Ferguson

In August 2000, Rangers went down 6-2 at Parkhead in a match that saw the Gers youngster sent off. After the game the midfielder was reportedly caught up in a street battle with Celtic fans – dubbed the 'Battle of Bothwell'.

11. Lorenzo Amoruso

After being sidelined with injury early in his Rangers career, the big Italian became frustrated at life sat at home. In his autobiography he reveals how he turned to drink to get him through the situation. "Anyone will tell you that drinking any kind of alcohol to excess is bad for you, but I was drinking something that not only made my head hurt but turned me into a fat slob. Not for me the usual bad things like whisky or vodka. No, I almost became addicted to Baileys!"

BERWICK AND OTHER NIGHTMARES

11 truly excruciating Rangers results

1. Berwick Rangers 1 Rangers 0 Scottish Cup, 28 January 1967
Sammy Reid scored the only goal in one of the biggest-ever Cup upsets. It was the first time the Gers had lost in the first round for 30 years. The hero on the day was Jock Wallace, the Berwick keeper, who would ironically later manage Rangers.

2. Rangers 0 Hamilton Academicals 1 Scottish Cup third round, 31 January 1987
Adrian Sprott scored the only goal of the game to send the Gers crashing out of the Cup – at Ibrox. The goal also ended Graeme Souness's hopes of landing the Treble in his first season in charge.

3. Dundee 6 Rangers 1 5 February 1938
This hammering at Dens Park was made all the worse by the fact that the Dark Blues went on to be relegated at the end of the season.

4. Motherwell 2 Rangers 1 Scottish Cup quarter-final replay, 12 March 1952
The Gers' hopes of lifting the Cup were destroyed by this defeat at Fir Park, but the club would go on to make amends by lifting the trophy the following year.

5. Celtic 7 Rangers 1 League Cup final, 19 October 1957
One of the club's heaviest defeats by their rivals on the biggest stage.

6. Rangers 0 Dumbarton 6 4 May 1892
The club's biggest league defeat.

7. Celtic 5 Rangers 1 21 November 1998
Doubles from Henrik Larsson and Lubo Moravcik sent the Hoops to an emphatic win. Scott Wilson's early dismissal didn't help matters.

8. Celtic 6 Rangers 2 27 August 2000
The day started badly – Chris Sutton put the Hoops ahead in the first minute – and it got steadily worse. Claudio Reyna and Billy Dodds salvaged some pride but Barry Ferguson's sending off nine minutes from time capped a very bad day at the office.

9. Rangers 3 Viktoria Zizkov 3 (on aggregate) UEFA Cup, 2002
There were few if any in the Rangers support who thought the Gers would have trouble making it past the Czech outfit. Even after the Light Blues had lost the first leg in Czechoslovakia 2-0, most thought they'd still make it through. After the Gers duly pulled the two goals back, the game at Ibrox went into extra time and the home side looked set to progress after Neil McCann put them 3-2 up. But the visitors equalised to go through on the away goals rule.

10. Aberdeen 6 Rangers 0 Scottish Cup semi-final, 10 April 1954
Losing to the men from the north is bad enough on any day, but a six-goal gubbing in the Cup is a little too much for anyone to take.

11. The Champions League 1995/96
Despite having players like Brian Laudrup and Paul Gascoigne, the Gers finished bottom of group C with just three points. They were beaten twice by Juventus, who went on to win the title, and also lost away at Steaua Bucharest. But much more was expected than draws against Steaua and in both games with Borussia Dortmund.

11 THE BATTLE OF BRITAIN (1992)

Goram

McCall   Robertson   Gough   McPherson

Brown   Gordon   Ferguson (Ian)   Durrant

Hateley   McCoist

The side that won the European Cup tie known as the 'Battle of Britain' v Leeds United, Elland Road, 2 November 1992. Rangers won 2-1.

BEST-EVER RANGERS XI…

A possible line-up. Please don't write in

1. Andy Goram

The Bury-born keeper joined Rangers for £1m from Hibs in 1991. A brilliant and agile goalkeeper, Andy probably had his best season in 1992/93 when Rangers went ten games unbeaten in Europe and lost just four games in the league in a Treble-winning year. His club record of 107 clean sheets in 258 games is unlikely ever to be beaten, although Stefan Klos has since done his best to wrestle the title of Rangers' best from the former Scotland No 1.

2. Sandy Jardine

Twice player of the year, Jardine was a reliable and consistent performer for the Gers in an eight-year spell that saw him win three league titles, five Scottish Cups, five League Cups and the Cup Winners' Cup in 1972. He was also a part of the Rangers team that lost to Bayern Munich in the final of the Cup Winners' Cup in 1967 and was widely praised by Franz Beckenbauer. He went on to play for Scotland in two World Cups, and was one of the stand-out performers in the 1974 competition. Jardine was a solid defender who offered the side attacking options from full-back.

He eventually moved to Hearts and, operating as sweeper, almost helped them to success in 1986 when they were runners-up in the league and the Scottish Cup.

3. John Greig

Quite simply, Mr Rangers. Greig has held almost every role bar tea lady since making his debut against Airdrie in 1961. He captained the side to the Cup Winners' Cup in 1972 and made 755 appearances for the club in total – the most by any player. He won five league titles, six Scottish Cups and four League Cups. When, after winning the Treble in 1978, Jock Wallace quit abruptly, Greig was handed the job. In his first season, the Gers almost repeated their Treble success, lifting both Cups but narrowly missing out on the title, finishing runners-up to Celtic. After leading the team to another League and Scottish Cup, Greig eventually quit in October 1983 after a poor start to the season. After seven years he returned in 1990 to work in the public relations department. He now works in youth development at Murray Park, looking to etch his name even deeper into the history of the club.

4. Terry Butcher

When the Englishman arrived at the club in 1986 along with fellow countryman Chris Woods (then reckoned to be one of the best keepers in England), it marked a major difference in the way the world would look at Rangers and signified a sea-change in the club's fortunes. Unbeknown to fans at the time, the pair would go on to lay the foundations of the club's epic nine-in-a-row triumph. Butcher was a commanding presence in the side of the late 1980s and a great leader on the pitch. He could always be relied upon to fight for the Rangers cause and won three league titles and two League Cups during his time at the club.

5. Richard Gough

One of three men who were involved in all of Rangers' nine-in-a-row triumphs, Gough was a superb leader on the park and a fierce competitor. He had been at Ibrox for trials as an 18-year-old but failed to impress the club's coaching staff and signed for Dundee United. The Gers soon realised their mistake and tried to bring the defender to Glasgow but he eventually moved to Spurs. After his short stint in London, Rangers finally got their man, signing him for £1m in 1987. Walter Smith described the Scotland international as "the cornerstone" of what was the most successful Rangers team of all time.

6. Jim Baxter

The Scot's time with Rangers wasn't perhaps as medal-bedecked as some of the others in this list, but he remains one of the most gifted footballers ever to pull on the light-blue jersey. Baxter had a sublime left foot and the touch of arrogance that all truly great players possess. The point was underlined when he sat on the ball during the 1963 Scottish Cup final showdown with Celtic. There were fall-outs over money during his time with the club, but Baxter's contributions on the field ensure that Slim Jim remains a true Rangers legend.

7. Paul Gascoigne

Gascoigne has carried baggage with him at every club throughout his career, and his time with Rangers was no exception. However, it's fair to say that no other team ever managed to get quite the same level of performance from the Englishman as the Gers did. In his three years in Glasgow he won two league titles, one Scottish Cup and a League Cup winner's medal, and formed a deadly midfield partnership with Brian Laudrup. Teams struggled to contain even one of them; stopping the pair was nigh-on impossible. In Europe, though, Gazza never quite did the biz.

8. Davie Cooper

Cooper could strike a ball every bit as firmly as Gers' other hard-hitting stars Jorg Albertz and Gio van Bronckhorst, but he combined that with a close control akin to that of Jim Baxter and the deftness of touch of Brian Laudrup. He won three league titles, three Scottish Cups and a staggering seven League Cups during his time with the club and contributed a string of memorable goals along the way. Davie died suddenly from a brain haemorrhage in 1995. He was only 39 and his premature passing shocked the whole country. It is testament to his standing in the game that when Rangers met another of his former teams, Motherwell, in the 2005 League Cup final, the event was renamed the Coop final in a tribute to the winger.

9. Brian Laudrup

The Dane joined the Gers in 1994 after an unhappy spell in Italy with Fiorentina and went on to become one of the club's most successful acquisitions. His header clinched the historic nine-in-a-row triumph in 1997, yet it is for his vision and close control that he will be most remembered for. Teams found him almost impossible to play against and his impact in Glasgow was underlined by the fact that, in a three-year spell, he was twice named the Football Writers' Player of the Year. Laudrup left for Chelsea in 1998, but it is fair to say that no other player has had such an impact in such a short space of time with the club.

10. Ally McCoist

Rarely scored spectacular strikes, but the sheer quantity of goals for Rangers ensures he will be one of the club's all-time greats. McCoist joined the Gers from Sunderland in 1983 – the club's third attempt at signing him. Ally finally started to become the idol he still is when he starred in the 1984 League Cup against Celtic, scoring a hat-trick in a 3-2 win. This was the start of a career that would see him net more than 300 goals in 500 appearances for Rangers. His best season came in 1992/93, like so many of the Rangers players on this list. That was the year Ally got more than 50 goals in league and cups, and he was the runaway winner of the Adidas European Golden Boot, a trophy given to strikers with the most goals in Europe at the end of the season. Ally made an emotional exit from Ibrox in 1998, but it wouldn't be a surprise if he comes back to Ibrox at some time as one of the staff.

11. Mark Hateley

Although the big Englishman wasn't an instant success at Ibrox, the former Monaco and Milan striker soon established himself as one of the most important players in the club's history. He netted 115 goals in a career with the club that saw him win five league titles, two Scottish Cups and three League Cups.

CAPTAINS COURAGEOUS

11 outstanding Ibrox leaders

1. George Young
2. Jock Shaw
3. Bobby Shearer
4. Eric Caldow
5. John Greig
6. Terry Butcher
7. Graham Roberts
8. Richard Gough
9. Lorenzo Amoruso
10. Barry Ferguson
11. Fernando Ricksen

CHEAP AT TWICE THE PRICE

Rangers 11 best imports

1. Brian Laudrup
2. Paul Gascoigne
3. Terry Butcher
4. Chris Woods
5. Mark Hateley
6. Stefan Klos
7. Alexei Mikhailichenko
8. Kai Johansen
9. Jean-Alain Boumsong
10. Arthur Numan
11. Ronald De Boer

CLOCKING UP THE AIRMILES

11 Rangers stars from furthest afield

1. Craig Moore Canterbury, Australia
The captain of Australia first spent time in Britain with Crystal Palace. He moved on to Germany with Borussia Moenchengladbach in January 2005, after being transfer-listed by Alex McLeish for putting the Athens Olympics before Rangers.

2. Bojan Djordjic Belgrade, former Yugoslavia
When war forces you to flee your country as a child, you grow up quickly. That might explain Mr Djordjic's confidence, some say cockiness, in front of the newspaper boys, from whom the Swedish under-21 cap won plaudits for his performances at press conferences. Now he just needs to repeat that flamboyance on the pitch.

3. Claudio Caniggia Henderson, Argentina
The striker arrived at Ibrox in 2001, via Ivano Bonnetti's attempted revolution at Dundee. Aged 34 (he had played in the 1990 World Cup final), he was hardly at his peak – indeed with his straggly blond hair he looked like something you might pick up in a Glasgow nightclub after one too many. But he had been a big hit at Dens Park and went on to contribute to the Gers Cup Double in 2002.

4. Andrei Kanchelskis Kirovograd, Ukraine
The wandering Ukrainian had already been to Manchester, Liverpool and Firenze by

the time he got to Glasgow in 1989. He'd move on to the other half of Manchester, Southampton and Saudi Arabia. No wonder he only had time for eight appearances.

5. Don Kitchenbrand Johannesburg, South Africa
Joined the Gers from South African club Delfos in 1955. The strong forward bagged 30 goals in just 37 games for the club before moving to Sunderland. His five goals in one game against Queen of the South in 1956 was a club record until surpassed by Davie Wilson's six against Falkirk in 1962.

6. Oleg Salenko St Petersburg, Russia
The man who scored five goals in a single World Cup match arrived at Ibrox in 1995 but failed to settle in Glasgow. He scored eight goals in 20 games before heading to Istanbulspor in Turkey.

7. Alexei Mikhailichenko Kiev, Ukraine
The winger arrived at Ibrox from Sampdoria in 1991 after helping the Italian outfit to their first Serie A title.

8. Oleg Kuznetsov Kiev, Ukraine
The defender arrived at Ibrox with an impressive reputation but an injury in only his second match meant he never really achieved that much in Glasgow.

9. Ben Ginzburg Tel Aviv, Israel
The Israeli international was understudy to Chris Woods after joining the club in 1989. He only made eight appearances for Rangers.

10. Avi Cohen Cairo, Egypt
Another Israeli international, Cohen had been a team-mate of boss Graeme Souness at Liverpool. International call-ups meant he only played 12 times for the club.

11. Gordan Petric Belgrade, former Yugoslavia
The defender joined Rangers from Dundee United. He cost the club £1.5m and went on to play 85 times.

CLOSER TO HOME

11 European countries who have provided Gers players

1. Sweden Joachim Bjorklund, Jonas Thern, Robert Prytz, Orjan Persson, Bojan Djordjic

2. Italy Lorenzo Amoruso, Sergio Porrini, Rino Gattuso, Marco Negri, Paulo Vanoli
3. Spain Mikel Arteta, Nacho Novo
4. Germany Stefan Klos, Jorg Albertz, Christian Nerlinger, Gerry Neef
5. France Basile Boli, Stephane Guivarc'h, Jean-Alain Boumsong, Gregory Vignal, Hamed Namouchi, Jerome Bonnissel
6. Iceland Therolf 'Tottie' Beck
7. Portugal Nuno Capucho
8. Norway Henning Berg, Tore Andre Flo, Egil Ostenstad
9. Greece Sotiris Kyrgiakos
10. Denmark Peter Lovenkrands, Erik Bo Anderson, Brian Laudrup, Jan Bartram, Erik Sorensen, Jorn Sorensen, Kai Johansen, Bajram Fetai
11. Belgium Thomas Buffel

COOP

11 magic ways to remember Davie Cooper

1. Rangers 2 Celtic 1 League Cup final replay, 18 March 1978
Cooper gave the Gers the lead in this tense replay. Celtic drew level through Edvaldsson, but Gordon Smith grabbed the winner. It was Coop's first League Cup winner's medal.

2. Rangers 3 Aberdeen 3 League Cup final, 25 October 1987
Cooper fired an unstoppable free kick past Jim Leighton to level the scores at 1-1. Four goals later, the game finished level but the Gers won on penalties, Cooper again hammering his shot past Leighton.

3. Rangers 3 Celtic 1 Dryburgh Cup final, 4 August 1979
In the final of this season-opening tournament, Cooper received the ball with his back to goal on the edge of the box. He flicked it into the air over one Celtic defender after another, beating four in total before volleying it into the goal. It was later voted the greatest-ever Rangers goal by fans.

4. Wales 1 Scotland 1 World Cup qualifier, 10 September 1985
Scotland needed a point from their World Cup qualifier in Cardiff to be sure of a place at the 1986 World Cup finals. Cooper scored the decisive spot kick to ensure his country would go to Mexico. It was a bittersweet moment, though: manager Jock Stein collapsed on the touchline shortly afterwards and died later in hospital.

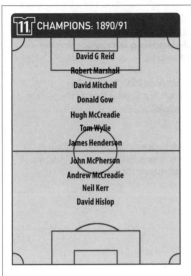

11. CHAMPIONS: 1890/91

David G Reid
Robert Marshall
David Mitchell
Donald Gow
Hugh McCreadie
Tom Wylie
James Henderson
John McPherson
Andrew McCreadie
Neil Kerr
David Hislop

The first Rangers XI to win the league title way back in 1890/91.

5. Rangers 4 Dundee United 1 Scottish Cup final replay, 12 May 1981
John Greig left Cooper on the bench for the original final but the mercurial winger played a pivotal role here as the Gers tore United apart, scoring one, setting up two.

6. Rangers 2 Celtic 1 League Cup final, 26 October 1986
Cooper fired home the winning penalty five minutes from the whistle to land Graeme Souness his first trophy as Rangers player/manager. His ice-cool kick capped a wonderful performance: throughout the game he'd turned Peter Grant and Murdo McLeod inside out.

7. Rangers 2 Dundee United 1 League Cup final, 28 November 1981
Coop was inspirational in a Rangers' fightback after Ralph Milne had given United the lead. He scored one and set up the other as Rangers lifted the Cup.

8. St Mirren 3 Rangers 3 17 September 1977
Coop latches on to Gordon Smith's knockdown to send a half-volley looping over the Paisley side's keeper. The goal was his first for the club since his switch from Clydebank and showed Gers supporters a glimpse of what was to come. Later in the game his cross set up Derek Johnstone for the Light Blues' second goal.

9. Rangers 2 Borussia Dortmund 0 UEFA Cup, 29 September 1982
After a goal-less first leg, Rangers knew victory on the night would see the club through to the second round. Cooper underlined his quality by opening the scoring before Derek Johnstone grabbed a second.

10. Rangers 1 Dundee United 0 League Cup final, 28 October 1984
Dave McPherson was named man of the match, but Cooper took all the plaudits as he picked up his fifth League Cup winner's medal.

11. Rangers 3 Celtic 2 10 September 1977
The Gers were 2-0 down at half time but with Cooper in inspirational form they fought back to win 3-2. He forced Hoops keeper Peter Latchford into two spectacular saves before setting up Derek Johnstone for the equaliser.

CUPS OF CHEER

Rangers' 11 biggest Cup final wins

1. **Rangers 5 St Mirren 0** 21 April 1934
2. **Rangers 5 Hearts 1** 18 May 1996
3. **Rangers 5 Dumbarton 1** 20 March 1897
4. **Rangers 4 Celtic 0** 4 April 1928
5. **Rangers 4 Aberdeen 0** 7 May 2000
6. **Rangers 4 Clyde 1** 3 April 1949
7. **Rangers 4 Dundee United 1** 12 May 1981
8. **Rangers 3 East Fife 0** 2 April 1950
9. **Rangers 3 Celtic 0** replay, 15 May 1963
10. **Rangers 3 Kilmarnock 0** 20 April 1932
11. **Rangers 3 Celtic 1** 2 April 1894

DEADLY DUOS

11 goal-grabbing Rangers partnerships

1. Jimmy Millar and Ralph Brand

Millar was a brave forward whose fantastic leap more than made up for his lack of height. The 5ft 6in Edinburgh man would often use his aerial prowess to set up Brand, a goal machine who bagged 206 in his time at Ibrox.

2. Ralph Brand and Don Kitchenbrand

South African Kitchenbrand was a bulky brute of a forward. He only played 37 times for the Gers but scored a staggering 30 goals.

3. Jim Forrest and Alec Willoughby

The cousins boasted two of the most impressive goals-per-games ratios the club has ever seen. Willoughby bagged 47 goals in 95 games while Forrest scored an amazing 163 times in just 145 games.

4. Derek Johnstone and Derek Parlane

Johnstone's biggest strength was in the air where he dominated defences. Parlane began as a midfielder but was converted into a striker by Jock Wallace. A shrewd move; he went on to bag 111 goals.

5. Derek Johnstone and Gordon Smith

Johnstone was one of the most versatile players in the club's history – he played in Cup finals for the Gers in defence, midfield and attack. Up front he formed an effective partnership with Smith. In the 1977/78 season they scored 63 goals between them.

6. Robert Fleck and Ally McCoist

Fleck provided an ideal partner for Ally McCoist. He was a strong player and bagged 34 goals before he was sold to Norwich City. His departure from Ibrox was seen as premature by fans but it was believed he had fallen out with the club over money.

7. Mark Hateley and Ally McCoist
Probably the most revered Gers' strike partnership. Hateley's dominance in the air enabled him to act as a great provider for McCoist, whose predatory instincts made him a nightmare for defenders.

8. Ally McCoist and Gordon Durie
With 355 goals during his time at Rangers, McCoist is without doubt the club's greatest striker. His partnership with Durie was similar in style to that with Hateley but Durie was more than just an aerial threat.

9. Rod Wallace and Michael Mols
A free transfer from Leeds United in 1998, Wallace made a valuable and unexpected impact on the Rangers team. He scored a number of crucial goals, including the winner in the 1999 Scottish Cup final. Mols showed a deftness of touch and had fantastic movement with or without the ball.

10. Tore Andre Flo and Michael Mols
Flo was (and often still is) criticised by the Rangers support. Although he did score goals for the club, they felt he never lived up to his staggering £12.5m transfer fee. Mols, in contrast, was a hugely popular player. He showed great ability in his early days at Ibrox, but a horrific injury incurred while playing against Bayern Munich in 1999 limited his development. He did eventually return to the team, but it was a case of what might have been for many Rangers fans, who felt he never fully recovered from the surgery.

11. Dado Prso and Nacho Novo
The pair have a long way to go before they're worthy of being called Rangers greats, but they have made an encouraging start since joining the club in the summer of 2004. They're the archetypal 'big man, little man' double act, with Novo providing blistering pace to complement Prso's imposing physical stature and eye for goal.

DEBUT GOALS
11 Rangers players who scored on their debut

1. Alexander Silcock-Smith
Bagged a hat-trick against Falkirk 9 March 1955.
2. Ralph Brand
Scored twice as Rangers beat Kilmarnock 6-0 on 6 November 1954.

3. Ian McMillan
Scored as Rangers drew 4-4 with Raith Rovers on 18 October 1958.

4. Harry Melrose
Scored two goals in the League Cup semi-final against Brechin City in his only game for Rangers on 28 September 1957. He went on to make his name with Dunfermline.

5. Derek Johnstone
Scored two against Cowdenbeath on 19 September 1970.

6. Shota Averladze
Scored twice in Rangers' 3-0 League Cup win over Airdrie on 9 October 2001.

7. Colin Stein
Scored a hat-trick against Arbroath on 2 November 1968, then repeated the feat a week later against his former club Hibs.

8. Stephane Guivarc'h
Looking back, it's hard to believe that the misfiring Frenchman scored at all during his time at Ibrox, but what's even more unbelievable is that he scored twice on his debut, bagging a brace in Rangers' 7-0 win at St Johnstone on 8 September 1998.

9. Rod Wallace
Rangers were 2-0 down to Hearts within 20 minutes at Tynecastle. Wallace, fresh from Leeds United, scored a debut goal just before the half hour but it wasn't enough to avoid defeat on 2 August 1998.

10. Chris Burke
Hit the back of the net in his first game, against Kilmarnock on 20 March 2002, as Rangers ran out 5-0 winners.

11. Steven Thompson
Scored eight minutes from time after coming on as a sub on 2 January 2003 against Dundee United – the team he'd just left.

COLIN STEIN SCORED A HAT-TRICK AGAINST ARBROATH, THEN REPEATED THE FEAT AGAINST HIBS

DEDICATED FOLLOWERS OF FASHION

11 Rangers players noted for their dress sense (or lack of it)

1. William Struth
Possibly the best-dressed man in the club's history. Struth was always immaculately turned out and pushed this philosophy on his players during his reign as manager. Bowler hats and spats were the in thing.

2. Jim Baxter
The midfielder's ability coupled with his partying lifestyle inevitably made him something of a trendsetter in Glasgow. Baxter was quick to sport the latest fashions. Alex Ferguson once likened him to Errol Flynn.

3. Davie White
White was the Gers' first tracksuit manager. A noticeable shift from his sartorially formal predecessors like Struth and Scot Symon.

4. Mark Hateley
If you could be sent to jail for crimes against fashion it's debatable how many goals the Englishman would have managed during his time at Ibrox. Some of the suits he sported were simply atrocious.

5. Terry Butcher
The England captain wasn't afraid of sporting the odd v-neck sweater. There was more than a hint of the Alan Partridge 'sports casual' look about him.

6. Paul Gascoigne
Although not averse to turning up for training in the nude, it wasn't his birthday suit that raised the most eyebrows. You name a colour – no matter how vivid – and Gazza was bound to own an all-in-one number in it.

7. Lorenzo Amoruso
Amo loved being the centre of attention and thrived on his celebrity status. The defender was a sharply dressed fellow (he was Italian, after all) but was guilty of occasional over-indulgence. He would often sport sunglasses on the top of his head (when it wasn't sunny) and once posed wearing only a Scotland flag for the papers.

8. Ferando Ricksen
The Dutchman isn't exactly the shy and retiring type and is quite happy in the spotlight. This might explain his diamond earring.

9. Marvin Andrews

The centre-back makes his mark in the Rangers fashion stakes. Gone are the designer suits of previous generations of Ibrox defenders. Andrews adopts the tracksuits and chains look, more akin to hip-hop stars than SPL footballers.

10. Dado Prso

The Croatian striker goes from one extreme to the other. He is either dressed like an extra from a war epic or spruced up to the nines ready for a night on the tiles.

11. Nacho Novo

Talk about toeing the party line! Judging by most snaps of the Spaniard away from the pitch, he must own every single piece of Rangers merchandise on offer. Rarely seen without a Rangers Union Jack baseball cap.

DEFENSIVE DUOS

11 double acts with real stopping power

1. Jock Shaw and George Young

Shaw and Young were invariably two of the first names on the Rangers team-sheet for a remarkable eight years between 1946 and 1952. The full-backs formed part of the Gers' famous 'Iron Curtain'.

2. John Greig and Ronnie McKinnon

The rock on which the Rangers teams of the 1960s and early 1970s were built. Greig was a leader on the pitch whilst centre-half McKinnon's composure on the ball had a reassuring effect on the rest of the team.

3. John Greig and Derek Johnstone

The versatile Johnstone made headlines as a striker but was also deployed in midfield and at centre-half during his time at Ibrox. He lined up at the back on numerous occasions, including the 1972 European triumph.

4. Tom Forysth and Colin Jackson

This pair provided Rangers with a solid base throughout much of the 1970s. Forsyth was a fearsome tackler, while centre-half Jackson was almost unbeatable in the air.

5. Craig Paterson and John McClelland

The duo played together from 1982-84. At a time when the Rangers team struggled in the league, the duo were key to the Gers achieving Cup success, winning two League Cups. Paterson captained the side to the 1985 League Cup victory.

6. Terry Butcher and Richard Gough
The Auld Enemy United for just short of three years at Ibrox. Although Gough could operate at right-back, it was his pairing with Butcher at the heart of the Rangers defence that was most impressive. Both had a strong physical presence, yet Gough in particular was more than comfortable with the ball at his feet.

7. Graham Roberts and Terry Butcher
Roberts deputised for Butcher when he was out with a broken leg in 1987/88 and also played alongside him. Both were fiercely competitive, willing to put everything on the line. Ironically the characteristics that made them so successful on the pitch probably contributed to them leaving Ibrox. Two strong personalities, they refused to back down after clashing with Graeme Souness: as a result, both were forced out.

8. Richard Gough and Dave McPherson
McPherson left to join Hearts in 1987 but returned to Ibrox five years later. There he teamed up with international team-mate Gough to form a solid base for much of Rangers' success of the period.

9. Richard Gough and Alan McLaren
McLaren joined Rangers in 1994 as one of the most promising players in the country. At a time when Rangers were looking to continue their run of success, they couldn't afford to allow players long periods to bed in. McLaren aided Gough and the other Rangers defenders by adapting quickly, showing pace and mobility.

10. Lorenzo Amoruso and Craig Moore
The Italian and the Australian were two mobile and capable defenders, yet neither offered the same reassurance that Gough had. After a rocky start, Amoruso became a popular figure with the Ibrox faithful, and still is, despite having left for the Premiership. Moore's popularity nose-dived after choosing to play in Australia's Olympic team rather than with Rangers in the summer of 2004. He did return to the first team but was eventually sold to Borussia Moenchengladbach.

11. Jean-Alain Boumsong and Marvin Andrews
This partnership developed nicely in the first half of the 2004/05 season. Boumsong dealt with the ball on the floor while Andrews was dominant in the air. Having the Frenchman alongside him seem to elevate the Trinidadian's game, something that became all the more noticeable when the French international moved to Newcastle.

DID THEY REALLY PLAY FOR RANGERS?

11 good reasons to install a revolving door at Ibrox

1. Daniel Prodan
The Romanian is part of Rangers' folklore. He joined the club from Atletico Madrid in the summer of 1998 but failed to make a single first-team appearance in two-and-a-half years because of injury.

2. Dragan Mladenovich
Joined the club in the summer of 2004 but was out the door on loan to Atletico Madrid by January 2005. Injuries hampered his attempts to forge a career at Ibrox but he also seemed bereft of both fitness and ability.

3. Stephane Guivarc'h
Scored twice on his debut after his switch to Glasgow from Newcastle United, but failed to deliver the quality you'd expect from a World Cup winner.

4. Emerson
The Brazilian was rumoured to be a target for Celtic before signing at Ibrox, but it was the Hoops' supporters who were laughing after the deal was done. The midfielder, who had commanded more than £12m in transfer fees before he arrived in Glasgow, wasn't at his petulant worst during his time with Rangers (happily he'd saved that for Middlesbrough) but he was truly woeful.

5. Sebastian Rozental
The first South American to play for Rangers joined the club from Chile's Universidad Cattolica for around £4m in 1997. Injury wrecked the striker's Ibrox career, though, and he failed to make a mark.

6. Ben Ginzburg
An Israeli international keeper who'd caught Graeme Souness's eye, Ginzburg arrived in 1989. However, when more transfer money was made available, Chris Woods was signed and 'Bonni' played only eight games for the Gers.

7. Duncan Ferguson
Much was expected when Ferguson arrived from Dundee United for £3.75m in 1993 but things went spectacularly wrong for the trouble-prone striker. The following April he was judged to have head-butted John McStay during a game against Raith Rovers. The referee didn't send him off but after the game the SFA decided the offence was worthy of a 12-game ban. As if that wasn't bad enough,

Glasgow's Procurator Fiscal charged the player with assault! Ferguson was already on probation and ended up with a three-month stretch in Barlinnie. After just 14 appearances and two goals he was sold to Everton for £4.4m that autumn.

8. Nuno Capucho

The Portuguese midfielder cost Rangers £670,000 in 2003 yet despite his international pedigree he never really impressed at Ibrox and a severance deal was agreed the following May.

9. Egil Ostenstad

The Norwegian was one of several purchases that could best be described as panic buys. The striker (who arrived from Blackburn Rovers) never looked to be of the quality required at Ibrox and only made four starts for the club.

10. Darius Adamczuk

The Polish international defender made only seven starts after his move from Dundee in 1999. He failed to impress boss Dick Advocaat and eventually moved on loan to Wigan Athletic in August 2001, more or less signalling the end of his career at Ibrox. Problems with depression didn't help and he was released in 2003.

11. Jean-Alain Boumsong

The big defender is different to the others on this list as his time at Ibrox was cut short because he was too good, rather than not good enough. When the French international arrived at Ibrox on a Bosman in the summer of 2004, most Rangers fans acknowledged that his quality probably meant he would move on eventually. However, few thought he'd last less than a season: after prolonged and increasing speculation, he joined Newcastle United for £8.5m that December. He was impressive during his spell at Rangers, winning over the media and fans alike. That said, shortly after his move to the north-east he confessed to having difficulties understanding the Scottish accent. Let's see how he gets on in Newcastle.

DID YOU KNOW?

11 unusual facts about Rangers players

1. Andy Goram's sporting prowess didn't stop at football: he also represented Scotland at cricket. He wasn't the first Ger to do this, though. Former boss **Scott Symon** was the first to represent Scotland on the football field and at the wicket.

2. Goram wasn't the only Gers star to have more than one string to his bow. **Tom Vallance**, who played for the club between 1874 and 1884, held the Scottish long jump record for 14 years and had two paintings in the Scottish Royal Academy.

3. Former Ibrox and England captain **Terry Butcher** was born in Singapore.

4. Former Celtic keeper **Alan Rough** almost became a Rangers player. Souness approached Rough about joining the club but the Ibrox board vetoed the transfer. The Gers went on to sign **Chris Woods** instead.

5. Former Ibrox winger **Willie Henderson** was famously short-sighted and had to wear contact lenses during games. Legend has it that he once went to the bench during an Old Firm game to ask how long was left. "Go and ask the other dugout, you bloody fool," was Jock Stein's reply. "This is the Celtic bench!"

6. Despite playing under the likes of Cesari Maldini and Carlo Ancelotti, Milan star **Rino Gattuso** counts Gers boss **Walter Smith** as the biggest influence on his career.

7. Former Rangers player (Sir) **Alex Ferguson** was a fierce union man while working on the Govan docks. He once sparked a walkout over working conditions.

8. **Davie Cooper** holds the record for League Cup wins. He won the trophy no fewer than seven times with Rangers. That's one more than Billy McNeill did for Celtic.

9. After losing 1-0 to Dynamo Kiev in the first leg of a European Cup match in 1987, **Graeme Souness** noticed that the Ukrainian outfit had continually used the flanks to great effect. To nullify this threat in the second leg, Souness ordered the Ibrox ground staff to bring in the touchlines and narrow the pitch. The dimensions still met UEFA rules and the Gers went through 2-1 on aggregate. UEFA has since changed the rules so clubs have to declare their pitch size before the start of the season.

> SOUNESS ORDERED THE GROUND STAFF TO NARROW THE PITCH... AND THE GERS WENT THROUGH 2-1

10. **Ally McCoist** scored a staggering 28 hat-tricks during his Rangers career.

11. Three players featured in all nine of Rangers' nine-in-a-row triumphs. They were **Ally McCoist**, **Richard Gough** and **Ian Ferguson**.

DOING THE DONS

11 great games with Aberdeen

1. Rangers 6 Aberdeen 1 5 October 1977
The Dons had run out 5-1 winners in the previous year's League Cup but this time a hat-trick from Gordon Smith and goals from Derek Johnstone, Alex Miller and Alex MacDonald ensured a comprehensive victory for the Gers.

2. Rangers 3 Aberdeen 1 28 April 1996
Paul Gascoigne scored a hat-trick as the Gers came from behind to clinch their 46th league title.

3. Rangers 2 Aberdeen 0 11 May 1991
The sides were neck-and-neck at the top of the league heading into the final game of the season. Mark Hateley scored twice to hand the Gers victory and the title.

4. Rangers 5 Aberdeen 0 21 January 2000
Craig Moore put the Gers ahead after 36 minutes and Gio van Bronckhorst doubled the advantage just two minutes later. The Light Blues went in 3-0 up before Rod Wallace and Barry Ferguson made it 5-0 by full-time.

5. Rangers 5 Aberdeen 0 21 October 2004
After a tight first-half, Rangers were just one up through Stevie Thompson. After the break it stayed close until Peter Lovenkrands added a second after 68 minutes. The Gers then added three more as Dons boss Jimmy Calderwood threw caution to the wind by playing four up front.

6. Rangers 4 Aberdeen 0 12 January 1997
It was easy for Rangers as Erik Bo Anderson bagged a double before goals from Jorg Albertz and Brian Laudrup completed the scoring.

7. Rangers 4 Aberdeen 0 4 September 1965
Spurred on by this early League Cup victory, the Gers went on to beat Celtic 2-1 in the final and lift the Cup.

8. Rangers 5 Aberdeen 1 21 February 1962
The Gers were 3-1 up by half time in this replay and pressed home their advantage after the break. This game was a far cry from the first match in this Scottish Cup tie, which had finished 2-2 at Pittodrie.

9. Rangers 6 Aberdeen 2 1 September 1906
The Gers picked up this emphatic First Division win after going down 2-0 at Port Glasgow the week before.

10. Rangers 5 Aberdeen 1 6 September 1913
Rangers went on to win the league by four points.

11. Rangers 5 Aberdeen 0 24 December 1927
The Gers spoiled Christmas for their rivals with an emphatic win at Ibrox.

DONE BY THE DONS

11 games against Aberdeen we'd sooner forget

1. Aberdeen 5 Rangers 1 19 January 1985
The first time Rangers had conceded five goals since the creation of the Premier Division. It's still Aberdeen's record Premier win.

2. Aberdeen 6 Rangers 1 18 April 1961
The Gers went on to win the title but almost threw it away with this hammering by Aberdeen (their record Scottish League win) and defeat by Killie the previous week.

3. Aberdeen 6 Rangers 0 Scottish Cup semi-final, 10 April 1954
Injuries on the day didn't help but the Gers conceded three in the last ten minutes as they crashed out of the Cup. And yes, it's Aberdeen's record Scottish Cup win.

4. Rangers 2 Aberdeen 3 27 April 1968
Rangers needed to beat the Dons and hope Dunfermline could beat Celtic if they were to pip their rivals to the title. The Gers lost their first game of the season here and with it the championship. It was their second successive trophy-less season.

5. Rangers 1 Aberdeen 4 Scottish Cup final, 22 May 1982
Rangers battled hard but current Ibrox boss Alex McLeish scored for the Dons to cancel out John MacDonald's opener. The game went to extra time and saw the Gers finally outplayed as they conceded three goals and the Cup.

6. Aberdeen 1 Rangers 0 Scottish Cup final, 21 May 1983
Lightning strikes twice as Rangers lose to Alex Ferguson's Aberdeen at the final hurdle for the second year in a row. Eric Black grabs the only goal.

7. Rangers 0 Aberdeen 3 13 May 1989
Rangers had won their first title in ten years (the first of nine in a row) three games earlier, so they might be forgiven for taking their foot off the gas. Still, not a memory to treasure.

8. Rangers 2 Aberdeen 4 17 September 1910
Despite this defeat at Ibrox, the Gers still managed to beat the Dons to the title. Rangers finished four points ahead of their rivals after our friends in the north drew ten of their 34 matches.

9. Aberdeen 3 Rangers 1 League Cup, 24 September 1980
After disposing of the Gers, the Dons were knocked out by Dundee in the next round. The Tayside outfit made it to the final but lost to their neighbours United 3-0.

10. Aberdeen 5 Rangers 1 League Cup, 27 October 1976
The Dons booked their place in the final by dishing out this drubbing. There they would beat Celtic 2-1 to lift the Cup, so at least Rangers lost to the eventual winners.

11. Aberdeen 4 Rangers 0 2 April 1955
The Dons went on to lift the title, with the Gers eight points behind in third spot.

DUTCH TREATS

Ten fine arrivals from the Netherlands – and Peter van Vossen

1. Dick Advocaat The Dutchman never played for the club but he was responsible for introducing a host of top names, many of whom happened to be Dutch.

2. Arthur Numan A cultured left-back who joined the club for £5m from PSV Eindhoven after the 1998 World Cup. He still appears in the Scottish media.

3. Bert Konterman The big defender (signed from Feyenoord in July 2000) took stick at times but he did score a 30-yard screamer against Celtic. Despite his varying performances in the light-blue jersey, he developed into something of a cult figure at Ibrox and always receives a rapturous welcome when he returns to the club.

4. Giovanni van Bronckhorst The Dutch international cost an eyebrow-raising £5.5m from Feyenoord in July 1998 but showed his obvious quality at Ibrox before moving to Arsenal, from where he moved on to Barcelona.

5. Michael Mols Signed from FC Utrecht for £4m in July 1999, the striker was a huge favourite at Rangers. He seemed to score goals for fun until a serious knee injury – picked up against Bayern Munich – took a massive toll on his career.

6. Fernando Ricksen A controversial character in the early stages of his Ibrox career, Ricksen (signed from AZ Alkmaar in July 2000 for £750,000) has matured in recent years. His new-found self-discipline and consistent performances have even seen him rewarded with the captain's armband. Supposedly named after the Abba song, Ricksen is hugely popular with supporters and is the one current Rangers player Celtic fans love to hate more than any other.

7. Ronald de Boer A regular Dutch international, midfielder de Boer signed for Rangers from Barcelona in September 2000 for £4.5m.

8. Frank de Boer The accomplished defender had a very brief spell at Ibrox in early 2004 – he probably only came to keep his brother company.

9. Ronald Waterreus The keeper arrived from Manchester City in January 2005 as cover for the injured Stefan Klos. Man of the match in his Old Firm debut at Parkhead.

10. Theo Snelders Back-up keeper to Andy Goram after joining from Aberdeen in 1996. Once refused to play in a Scottish Cup quarter-final match.

11. Peter van Vossen Arrived at Ibrox as part of the deal that saw Oleg Salenko head to Istanbulspor in January 1996. Sadly for the striker, his time in Glasgow is probably best remembered for a spectacular miss against Celtic. He was unmarked, just feet from the line, but somehow scooped the ball over the bar.

EASTERN DELIGHTS

11 great Gers from Enbra and beyond

1. Ralph Brand
Brand was born in Edinburgh but signed pro forms with Rangers in 1954. Despite having to do two years' national service, he still went on to make 317 appearances for the club. A prolific scorer, he went on to play for Manchester City, Sunderland and Raith Rovers. He is the only player to score in three successive Scottish Cup finals.

2. Graeme Souness
Headed south to Spurs in 1970 arriving at Rangers in 1986 (via Middlesbrough, Liverpool and Sampdoria) as player-manager. Won the title in his first season.

3. John Greig
Edinburgh-born but now sewn into the fabric of Glasgow Rangers. Indeed, he was once named The Greatest Ranger in a fans' poll. Twice player of the year, he made 857 appearances for the Gers, notching up 142 goals along the way. He captained and then managed the side.

4. Alan McLaren
His career was cut short by injury aged only 27, but the full-back still managed a fair share of silverware in his short time at Ibrox. The defender played just short of 100 games and won two championships, including the final success in the side's nine-in-a-row triumph, and a Scottish Cup.

5. Willie Woodburn
The short-fused centre-half was famous for being the last player in Britain to be handed a *sine die* (indefinite) ban. He was handed the hefty sentence as punishment for headbutting a Stirling Albion player. At the time (1954), many believed that he was being used as an example to deter others from losing their temper on the pitch.

11 EUROPEAN CUP WINNERS' CUP FINAL

Ritchie

Shearer
Davis   Paterson   Caldow

McMillan   Baxter

Scott   Wilson   Brand   Hume

**The first Scottish team to reach a European final.
Cup Winners' Cup final
v Fiorentina
17 and 27 May 1961.
Lost 1-4 (on aggregate).**

The ban was overturned almost three seasons later but Woodburn's career was over. This well-publicised moment of ill-discipline overshadowed the fact that he was an accomplished, ball-playing centre-back at a time when few defenders were comfortable with the ball at their feet.

6. David Hagen
Signed as a 13-year-old, Hagen showed promise as an old-fashioned winger but made only 20 appearances before moving back east to join Hearts.

7. Sandy Robertson
Spent seven years at Ibrox, making his debut in the benefit match for victims of the 1988 Lockerbie bombing. Robertson showed great ability but his Rangers career was hampered by the club's policy of importing expensive foreign stars. As a result he only managed 30 games in the light-blue jersey.

8. Sandy Jardine
One of the club's greatest-ever players, Jardine excelled in a number of positions but will be most remembered for his performances at full-back. On his international debut he marked Eusébio out of the game.

EUROPEAN TRIUMPH V DYNAMO MOSCOW 1972

McCloy

Jardine Greig Johnstone Mathieson

Smith

MacDonald

Conn Johnston

McLean Stein

Rangers finally achieve European glory in the Cup Winners' Cup final , beating Dynamo Moscow, a triumph marred by a year ban from European football after Gers fans invaded the pitch.

9. Alfie Conn

Remembered for a powerful right-foot shot, the Kirkcaldy-born player played 149 games for Rangers before switching to Spurs. After a spell in England he shocked Rangers fans in 1977 by signing for Celtic. To make matters worse, he went on to win the Scottish Cup with the Hoops later that year – against Rangers.

10. Martin Henderson

Another Kirkcaldy-born Ger, the centre-forward played almost 50 times for the club, netting 14 goals along the way. He sometimes struggled to maintain form but was an important player in the Treble-winning 1975/76 season, bagging some vital goals.

11. Craig Paterson

Born in South Queensferry, the big defender joined the Gers from Hibs in 1982. Injuries and loss of form hampered his Rangers career at times but he can still boast captaining the side in the 1984/85 League Cup triumph. After leaving Ibrox he moved to Motherwell, helping the Lanarkshire side to the Scottish Cup in 1991.

EUROPEAN DISASTERS

Those of a sensitive disposition should look away now

1. Bayern Munich 1 Rangers 0 Cup Winners' Cup final, 31 May 1967
Rangers took on a Munich side packed with stars like Sepp Maier, Franz Beckenbauer and Gerd Müller. To make the task even more difficult, the match was staged in the Germans' backyard, in Nuremberg. The Gers battled hard and had a goal disallowed, but eventually lost in extra time. It was the first season in 15 years that the Light Blues had finished without a trophy. To make matters worse, Celtic had become the first British team to lift the European Cup six days earlier.

2. Eintracht Frankfurt 6 Rangers 1 European Cup, 13 April 1960
The German side outclassed Rangers as they all but booked their place in the final.

3. Rangers 3 Eintracht Frankfurt 6 European Cup, 5 May 1960
All hopes of salvaging some pride from their first-leg encounter were blown out of the water as the visitors fired six past the beleaguered Rangers' defence.

4. Rangers 3 Viktoria Zizkov 3 (aggregate score) UEFA Cup, 2002
Rangers went down 2-0 in the first leg in Prague. But when the Czech side came to Ibrox, Ronald de Boer scored twice to send the match into extra-time. Thirty minutes later it was 3-1 on the night and the Gers were out on away goals.

5. Fiorentina 2 Rangers 1 (4-1 on aggregate) Cup Winners' Cup, 27 May 1961
The Gers missed the chance to win the very first Cup Winners' Cup after being outplayed by the Italians over the two legs.

6. Rangers 0 AEK Athens 1 European Cup, qualifying round second leg, 24 August 1994
The Gers were two-nil down after the first leg in Greece and failed to take their chances in this leg at Ibrox. To make matters worse, the Greek side grabbed a breakaway goal to win in Glasgow, too. Overall, Greeks 3 Geeks 0.

7. Tottenham Hotspur 5 Rangers 2 Cup Winners' Cup, 31 October 1962
The Gers were outclassed by a London side featuring a forward line that included Jimmy Greaves, Les Allen and John White. The Gers battled hard in the return leg at Ibrox but went down 8-4 on aggregate. Spurs went on to win the trophy.

8. Real Madrid 6 Rangers 0 European Cup, 9 October 1963
A young Rangers side was outplayed by a Madrid outfit boasting the likes of Ferenc

EUROPEAN HEROES

McCloy

Caldow   Greig   Jardine

McKinnon   Johnstone

Baxter

Johnston

Millar   McCoist   Hateley

An all-purpose Gers XI all of whom represent talented variations on a single theme: they have been Light Blue heroes in Europe. Bit of a void in midfield but Ronnie McKinnon was so effective against Alfredo di Stefano in September 1963, it's impossible to omit him.

Puskas, Alfredo Di Stefano and Paco Gento. After the Light Blues missed an early chance to go ahead, Puskas went on to score a hat-trick in a rout by the Spanish side.

9. Manchester United 3 Rangers 0 Champions League, 4 November 2003
The Gers travelled hoping to repeat the success of their last trip south in European competition when they beat Leeds United 2-1 at Elland Road in 1992. Things didn't quite work out: Ruud van Nistelrooy scored twice and Diego Forlan scored the third.

10. Grasshoppers Zurich 3 Rangers 0 Champions League, 11 September 1996
Despite fielding a full-strength side including star names such as Gascoigne and Laudrup, Rangers struggled against their Swiss hosts and were 1-0 down after only 18 minutes. The 3-0 defeat meant a hard start to life in group A. They never recovered and failed to progress to the next round.

11. Rangers 0 Juventus 4 Champions League, 1 November 1995
After going down 4-1 in the first leg, Rangers were hoping to restore some pride in Glasgow. Matters didn't go exactly to plan though as Del Piero, Marocchi, Toricelli and Ravanelli scored for the visitors. The only consolation for the Ibrox faithful was that Juve went on to win the tournament with victory over Ajax in the final.

EUROPEAN JOYS

That's more like it!

1. Rangers 3 Dynamo Moscow 2 Cup Winners' Cup final, 24 May 1972
Four minutes into the second-half Rangers were three goals up, following one strike from Colin Stein and two from Willie Johnston. The Gers looked to be heading towards a comfortable victory but the Russians scored on the hour and grabbed a second three minutes from time. The Rangers fans packed into the Nou Camp had a nervous wait but the side held on to lift the trophy.

2. Rangers 2 Bayern Munich 0 Cup Winners' Cup semi-final, 19 April 1972
Sandy Jardine's cross eluded goalkeeper Sepp Maier to give the Gers a first-minute lead. Derek Parlane added a second, enough to see the Light Blues into their third Cup Winners' Cup final.

3. Rangers 3 Sporting Lisbon 4 Cup Winners' Cup second round, 3 November 1971
With the aggregate scores level 6-6, Rangers entered a penalty shoot-out against Sporting Lisbon, missed all three penalties and still went through. Why? Because the ref forgot the away goals rule. To be fair to Dutch referee Van Ravens, the rule was pretty new and even the players forgot it applied. John Greig recalls, "We were pretty disconsolate in the bath when John Fairgrieves, a journalist on the *Sunday Mail*, rushed in and pointed out that, under the new rules, we had scored three away goals to their two and should have won. Fairgrieves' view was confirmed by UEFA who suspended the referee. After that, the Gers felt their name really was on the trophy.

4. PSG 0 Rangers 0 (4-3 pens) UEFA Cup, December 2001
In a tense night in Paris, Rangers overcame a French side including Nicolas Anelka, Jay-Jay Okocha and Ronaldinho to reach the fourth round on penalties – the first Rangers side in over nine years to be still in Europe after Christmas.

5. PSV Eindhoven 2 Rangers 3 European Cup, 1 November 1978
The first leg finished 0-0 and most had written off the Gers chances. The pundits looked to have got it right when the Dutch scored after only 34 seconds but Alex MacDonald drew the Gers level. PSV went ahead again but Derek Johnstone levelled the scores. With only three minutes to go, Bobby Russell scored to send Rangers through. This was PSV's first-ever defeat at home in Europe.

6. Leeds United 1 Rangers 2 European Cup, 4 November 1992
Few in the English press gave Rangers any hope of progressing, despite the 2-1 lead from the first leg. But in a pulsating game, Mark Hateley hit a spectacular 25-yard

shot on the turn which looped over John Lukic in the Leeds goal. United came roaring back but Gers keeper Andy Goram was in inspired form. As the Yorkshire side pushed forward Rangers were able to hit them on the break, and on one of these occasions Mark Hateley broke down the left and crossed for Ally McCoist to head home. Eric Cantona scored late on for the home side but it was Rangers who went through.

7. Rangers 2 Dynamo Kiev 0 (2-1 on aggregate) European Cup, 30 September 1987
Rangers came back from the first leg 1-0 down – to a goal scored by future Gers player Alexei Mikhailichenko in front of a crowd of 100,000. Mark Falco put the Light Blues ahead before Ally McCoist headed the winner 20 minutes from time.

8. Rangers 2 Parma 0 European Cup, 11 August 1999
Tony Vidmar and Claudio Reyna were on target as the Gers beat the Italian giants in Glasgow. The Serie A side included such star names as Lillian Thuram, Dino Baggio, Ariel Ortega and Gianluigi Buffon.

9. Rangers 10 Valletta 0 (18-0 on aggregate) Cup Winners' Cup, 28 September 1983
The first time the Gers had scored 10 goals in a single European match. John McDonald bagged a hat-trick against the Maltese minnows.

10. Sparta Rotterdam 2 Rangers 3 European Cup, 9 March 1960
Falkirk-born Max Murray was among the scorers as the Gers recorded an impressive away win in front of 50,000 fans. At the time, Sparta Rotterdam were a force to be reckoned with.

11. Rangers 3 Rapid Vienna 3 21 January 1933
It may have only been a friendly match but Rapid Vienna were the first foreign side to visit Ibrox. Some 56,000 saw the six-goal thriller.

FAMOUS FANS

11 celebrity supporters of varying blue hues

1. Jonathan Watson
The comedian and impersonator is a big Rangers fan, but even the most ardent Celtic supporter would admit that he gives both teams an equally hard time when filming *Only An Excuse*.

2. Colin Montgomerie
Scotland's top golfer is a fan, although he's also alleged to support Leeds.

3. Patsy Kensit
Claimed to be a Rangers fan whilst appearing on *Fantasy Football League* in the early 1990s (bet that went down well with her one-time hubby, Hoops-fanatic Jim Kerr).

4. Robert Carlyle
Usually cited as a Gers fan in cyberspace but with no hard evidence. He refuses to discuss the matter but did once claim that what Rangers paid Gazza could keep Partick Thistle's team in some comfort – so we're guessing he's not. We would, of course, be happy to be proven wrong.

5. Gordon Ramsay
The hot-tempered chef was on Rangers' books until the age of 18, but never fully recovered from a cartilage injury and was released.

6. Andy 'The Viking' Fordham
If the Rangers players needed any further incentive to beat Celtic, keeping this 20-stone darts champion happy could well be it.

7. Midge Ure
The former Ultravox front man and Band Aid organiser is reputed to be a big fan of the Light Blues.

8. Nick Nairn
The pies at Ibrox are pretty good but it's nice to know there's someone waiting in the wings if the Gers need a hand in the kitchen.

9. Carol Smilie
Next time Ibrox needs sprucing up we know who to call.

10. Alan McGee
Founder of Creation records and discoverer of Oasis.

11. Kenneth Branagh
Ken claims to be a big fan of Rangers, Spurs and Linfield, but he has also gone on record as saying what a great dribbler of the ball Stuart Pearce was.

FINAL COUNTDOWN

11 of Rangers' finest domestic cup finals

1. Rangers 2 Aberdeen 1 Scottish Cup, 29 May 1993
Mark Hateley and Neil Murray grabbed the goals as the Gers lifted the Cup and completed a domestic Treble. Victory was made all the sweeter as refurbishment work at Hampden meant the match was staged at Celtic Park, home of their rivals.

2. Rangers 5 Hearts 1 Scottish Cup, 18 May 1996
Gordon Durie bagged a hat-trick but it was two-goal Brian Laudrup who inspired Rangers to victory. The Gers were simply irresistible as they lifted the trophy with an emphatic win. It was the Light Blues' 14th domestic Double and Paul Gascoigne became the third Englishman to win both the Scottish and English FA Cups.

3. Hearts 0 Rangers 2 Scottish Cup final second replay, 25 April 1903
Rangers took the lead after 15 minutes but from that point had to withstand fierce pressure. Their cause wasn't helped as they were reduced to ten men but the Light Blues held on and eventually grabbed a second to ensure the Cup headed to Ibrox.

4. Rangers 2 Aberdeen 1 League Cup, 31 March 1979
The Gers went behind 15 minutes into the second-half but levelled with 15 minutes to go. In the dying moments of the match, centre-half Colin Jackson rose to head the winner – the result sent Rangers on their way to completing the domestic Double.

5. Rangers 3 Celtic 2 League Cup, 25 March 1984
John Greig had stepped down as Rangers' manager earlier in the season so the Gers were led out by Jock Wallace. Ally McCoist scored twice after the break to put them 2-0 up, but Celtic came back and Mark Reid levelled in the dying seconds of normal time. As the first period of extra time was drawing to a close, McCoist was brought down by Roy Aitken; Rangers had a penalty. Adding to the drama, McCoist's effort was saved, but he scored from the rebound, sending Rangers on to victory.

6. Rangers 2 Aberdeen 1 League Cup, 25 October 1992
The Gers went into the game on the back of a gruelling Champions League match with Leeds United. Stuart McCall opened the scoring for Walter Smith's side but Duncan Shearer levelled things for the Dons midway through the second-half. The game went into extra-time but Rangers went on to lift the Cup after Mark Hateley pressured Gary Smith into an own goal.

7. Rangers 1 Celtic 0 Scottish Cup final replay, 27 April 1966
The Hoops were favourites to lift the Cup after the goal-less first encounter – Jock Stein had built a formidable side, who would win the European Cup the following season. However the Gers battled hard and grabbed a winning goal from an unlikely source – Danish full-back Kai Johansen. He only scored nine times in his Ibrox career, and this goal was undoubtedly his most important.

8. Rangers 2 Celtic 1 League Cup, 1986/87
A thriller saw chances at both ends before Davie Cooper's spot kick sealed victory.

9. Rangers 3 Celtic 2 Scottish Cup, 2002
Celtic took the lead twice but the Gers fought back each time through goals from Peter Lovenkrands and Barry Ferguson. The match was two minutes into injury time when Lovenkrands met Neil McCann's cross to seal a dramatic victory.

10. Rangers 3 Aberdeen 3 (6-5 on penalties) League Cup, 25 October 1987
Davie Cooper, Ian Durrant and Robert Fleck scored in a seesaw 90 minutes before the Gers finally won the match on penalties.

11. Rangers 3 Aberdeen 2 League Cup, 23 October 1988
Ally McCoist added to his earlier penalty when he scored a dramatic last-minute winner for the Gers.

GAZZA: THERE'S ONLY ONE PAUL GASCOIGNE…

Sometimes it's just as well. Here are 11 defining Gazza moments

1. In the League Cup final of 1996, Ally McCoist had put Rangers two goals up before Hearts levelled before the break. Frustration started to get the better of some players and Gazza was involved in an on-pitch bust-up with McCoist. After half-time, however, he emerged in inspired form and dragged the Gers to a 4-3 victory. He scored his first from 18 yards before playing a one-two with Charlie Miller to get Rangers' winner.

2. Midway through Rangers' 7-0 trouncing of Hibs on 30 December 1995, Gascoigne spotted the referee had dropped his yellow card. Picking it up, Gazza first pretended to book himself, then to book the official before handing him back his card with a smile. Everyone in Ibrox took it as a joke – except ref Dougie Smith who took the card and really did book the Rangers star. And referees wonder why no one likes them…

3. During his time at Rangers, Gazza was the subject of a documentary. Early in the shoot he led the crew up to the door of a quaint cottage which he informed them was his new pad. When they got there, he pretended he'd lost his keys and knocked instead. When a woman opened the door, Gazza launched into his very best Danny Baker impression asking the confused housewife whether she preferred Daz or Omo.

4. Training is not the most popular part of a professional footballer's life – pounding round the pitch can be a little boring. However, few footballers would choose to relieve the tedium in quite the same way as Gazza. After a heavy run around with the Rangers first-team squad, he decided it would be funny to stand over team-mate Erik Bo Anderson and urinate from a great height. Surprisingly, the Dane took the incident quite well. It's fair to say most professional footballers wouldn't.

5. After a day out fishing, Gazza thought he'd play a prank on his team-mate Gordon Durie. Whilst the striker was busy, Gascoigne went about hiding a trout in his car.

After driving round for weeks wondering what the smell was, Durie eventually worked out what had happened and found the fish concealed in his spare wheel. Thinking that was that, Durie had the car cleaned and went about his business. It soon became very clear that the smell was still there, however. It turned out Gazza had taken things that little bit further. He'd dismantled the back seat of the car and hidden another fish inside.

6. One Christmas a number of Rangers' directors were entertaining potential sponsors at Ibrox. They were above the home dressing-room and after a short while the sound of Christmas carols came drifting up the stairs. The culprit was Gazza. He was asked to keep it down and for about ten minutes all was well. Then the songs started up again, only this time louder. Officials made their way downstairs to find Gazza, accompanied this time by a full choir of ground staff and tea ladies.

7. On another occasion, Gazza injured his ankle and went to the Ibrox treatment room to have it put in plaster. The club physio spent ages, meticulously ensuring that everything was right and that it would set properly. After finishing the job the medic asked Gazza how it felt, to which the midfielder replied: "That's fantastic, you've done a great job. There's just one thing… it's the other ankle I twisted!"

8. Gazza was one of the few players to befriend Rangers' Russian signing, Oleg Salenko, bought on the strength of a single five-goal game against Cameroon in USA 94. The Russian, who got paid in cash and kept his wages under his bed, used to take Gazza on, in flare-gun fights. When Salenko was sold, Gazza began to find the solitude on Loch Lomond oppressive.

9. When Gazza scored his wonder goal for England against Scotland at Wembley in Euro 96, fights broke out among the Scottish fans because some Rangers supporters felt compelled to cheer a stroke of genius from a player they revered while others took heated exception to the cheering.

10. During match days at Ibrox, the crowd are entertained by the club's mascot, Broxi Bear. The furry performer dances and jigs his way around the pitch before matches, lifting the atmosphere and delighting the team's younger followers. It was possible for fans to hire the costume and play Broxi for the day. On one occasion in the mid-1990s, the wife of a local businessman handed over a considerable sum for her husband to have the privilege. On the day, Gascoigne was warming up with the other players when one told him that Richard Gough was inside the costume. Gazza proceeded to rugby tackle Broxi, repeatedly "putting the boot in" while laughing as his 'captain' squirmed on the floor.

11. One of the highlights of Gazza's Ibrox sojourn was meeting Sean Connery. An over-awed Gascoigne met the former 007 at a pre-season tournament. The two shook hands – the footballer speculating how many women those hands had caressed – and Gazza said: "You're bigger than I thought", to which Connery replied: "Always".

GOT YOU UNDER MY SKIN

11 players fans love to hate

1. Bertie Auld
The midfielder was part of the 1967 Lisbon Lions team, which in itself probably rankles with many Rangers fans. A confident, irrepressible character on the Celtic teams of yore and a player imbued with a great self-belief, he had a tigerish, never-say-die attitude which made him a frustrating opponent for the Gers.

2. Alfie Conn
After leaving Ibrox for a stint down south, Conn returned to Glasgow – with Celtic.

3. Tommy Gemmell
The Scotland international was a tough-tackling player and was involved in more than his fair share of bruising encounters with Rangers.

4. Peter Grant
Part of the Celtic team that had to endure Rangers' nine-in-a-row triumph, Grant was never one to shirk a tackle and his dedication to the cause made him a target for abuse. He was happy to wind up the Gers support even after leaving the club, criticising Henning Berg when he spoke out against Alex McLeish in 2004. It was nothing to do with him, but Grant was happy to stick his oar in nevertheless.

5. Roy Aitken
Another forceful character, midfielder Aitken was one Celt who really riled Rangers fans. He didn't always have it his own way on the pitch against Rangers, though. The Gers faithful savoured the 1984 League Cup final. Aitken brought down Ally McCoist for a penalty in injury time. Ally missed at the first attempt but scored from the rebound to win the Cup.

6. Frank McAvennie
One of the most, erm, colourful characters to have played in Scotland, McAvennie

wasn't exactly a hate figure for the Gers support. But the St Mirren and Celtic striker bagged his fair share of goals against the club and was therefore a popular target for their frustrations. Sadly for them, Frank was the kind of player who thrived on this kind of attention.

7. Neil Simpson

While playing for Aberdeen, Simpson severely damaged the knee of Rangers' midfield star Ian Durrant in an horrific studs-up tackle. Durrant was forced to spend two years out recovering. Simpson has never been forgiven for the tackle.

8. Henrik Larsson

Not a dirty player or a cheat, but disliked simply for the damage he did to Rangers. Many supporters will wonder how many more trophies the Gers might have won if the Hoops had been stripped of their talismanic Swede.

9. Alan Thompson

In fairness to the Celt, a series of good performances against the Gers are the main reason for his unpopularity, although his long-running feud with Fernando Ricksen probably hasn't helped. The pair haven't seen eye-to-eye throughout their time in Scotland. After tangling on the pitch a number of times, Ricksen (who lived near Thompson) allegedly banged on Thommo's front door and shouted through the letterbox after a 2002 Old Firm game. Thompson, meanwhile, enraged the Rangers support by landing a playful slap on Ricksen's face during the celebrations after Chris Sutton's last-minute winner at Parkhead in 2004. The pair have kept their emotions in check lately, but tension remains.

10. Neil Lennon

A Catholic from Northern Ireland, the midfielder has been the target of boo-boys throughout his career for his tigerish displays, but never as much as in Glasgow. After being on the receiving end of abuse throughout one Old Firm game at Ibrox, Martin O'Neill even marched him to the Celtic end to take a bow.

11. Craig Bellamy

Very quickly overtaking Lennon as the least popular player in the current Celtic squad. Has yet to have any direct run-ins with the Gers, but one senses it's only a matter of time if he stays on. Boasting about his wages to Clyde players and refusing to shake hands with Hibs' Gary Caldwell after a game, has already alienated large sections of Scotland's football supporters.

GREAT GAFFERS

Actually, the club has only had 11 managers, so here they all are

1. William Wilton 1899-1920

Wilton took on the dual role of manager and secretary in May 1899 but he'd already been at the club for 16 years. In the days before managers, Wilton held various roles, allowing senior first-team members to dictate tactics. During that time the squad picked up two Scottish championships and three Scottish Cups. After taking this new role, he guided the club to their first 100-per-cent league record and a further seven league championships. He drowned in a boating accident in May 1920.

2. William Struth 1920-54

In 34 years at the club Struth established what it meant to play for Glasgow Rangers. He ensured that his players appeared smart at all times, encouraging them to sport bowler hats and spats. He kept more than half-a-dozen double-breasted suits in his office and would often change two or three times a day. During his reign the club won 18 league championships, including 14 in 19 years. The team also recorded the first league and Cup Double in 1928, and the club's first Treble in 1949.

3. Scot Symon 1954-67

Symon had played under Struth and worked hard to carry on his traditions. He led the club to six league championships and back-to-back Doubles in 1963 and 1964. Symon was the first man to take the club into Europe, reaching two European finals, in 1961 and 1967. Before Rangers, he had managed East Fife and Preston North End, coaching the legendary Tom Finney. Symon was sacked in 1967 after rejecting the offer of being pushed upstairs to become general manager.

4. Davie White 1967-69

White was brought to the club from Clyde to be groomed as Symon's successor but when Symon left, he was thrown into the hot seat after just five months. It came too soon for the tracksuited former wing-half and he holds the unfortunate honour of being the only manager not to win any silverware. In fairness to White, he was up against it. The Celtic side of the day were hugely dominant, but it was often suggested that he had trouble dealing with star names and that he was almost in awe of players like Jim Baxter. He was sacked after defeat to Polish side Gornik.

5. Willie Waddell 1969-72

After retiring as a player in 1956, the former Rangers star took over at Kilmarnock and guided them to their first and only league title in 1965. After a brief spell as a journalist, he returned to Ibrox in 1969 to succeed the unfortunate Davie White.

He led the side to the League Cup in 1971 – their first trophy in five years – then guided the club through one of its darkest hours: the Ibrox stadium tragedy in 1971. Sixty-six people lost their lives. Waddell made sure the club was represented at each of the victim's funerals. He then went on to oversee the redevelopment of the ground, ensuring that safety was a priority. He was still able to guide the side to one of their most memorable achievements – lifting the Cup Winners' Cup in 1972. Later that year he moved upstairs and handed control to his assistant, Jock Wallace.

6. Jock Wallace 1972-78 and 1983-86
Hardened by spells with the King's Own Scottish Borderers, the big former keeper was a fantastic motivator. He had served in Northern Ireland and fought in the jungles of Malaysia, so he was ready to impose his identity on the club. His teams had tremendous fitness and he led the team to the title in 1975 – the club's first in 11 years. Wallace's side went on to win the Treble in 1976 and again in 1978. He was the first manager in Scotland to guide a team to two domestic Trebles but quit shortly after the second. He returned five years later, winning two League Cups but lack of success in the league saw him leave for a second time in 1986.

7. John Greig 1978-83
Greig had been inspirational on the pitch and, with Wallace's decision to leave, he had the chance to inspire the team off it, too. He epitomised Rangers' fighting spirit and was quick to rise to the challenge. In his first season, the team narrowly missed out on the Treble, winning the Scottish and League Cups but finishing second in the title race. He guided the team to another League Cup in 1982 and the Scottish Cup in 1981 but quit the post in 1983.

8. Graeme Souness 1986-91
Souness's arrival brought about the 'Souness Revolution' as he set about dragging Rangers back to the top of the table. Under his charge, the club bought established international players and reversed the trend of talent heading south. He built his team around such seasoned stars as Terry Butcher and Chris Woods, and his policy was proved right as he lifted the championship and League Cup in his first season. He steered them to two more league titles and two more League Cups, but, with the Gers sitting top of the table with just five games left, quit to return to Liverpool.

9. Walter Smith 1991-98
Smith picked up where his former boss Souness had left off and steered the club to arguably their greatest achievement – nine successive league titles (six under his guidance). He did this by building on the squad established in the previous five years, adding players like Andy Goram, Stuart McCall and, later, Paul Gascoigne and

Brian Laudrup. But his most important decision was to show faith in McCoist, out of favour under Souness. Rangers won the League and Cup Double in Smith's first season and the Treble a year later, also narrowly missing out on the European Cup final. Smith quit the club in 1998, enduring a mediocre spell as boss of Everton before returning as Scotland's national coach.

10. Dick Advocaat 1998-2002

The Little General arrived at Ibrox after guiding PSV to the Dutch championship and Dutch Cup in 1996, having earlier led Holland to the quarter-finals of the 1994 World Cup. Advocaat reshaped the team with players like Gough, Goram and McCoist replaced by Arthur Numan, Giovanni van Bronckhorst and Andrei Kanchelskis. The Light Blues won the domestic Treble in his first season, clinching the league title with victory at Celtic Park. The team won the Double the following year, finishing 21 points ahead of second-placed Celtic. Advocaat became director of football in 2002 before leaving for a second stint in charge of the Dutch national side.

11. Alex McLeish 2002-

A naturally humorous man, the former Motherwell and Hibs manager is more guarded in his answers now that he's under the Old Firm microscope. That said, he's a personable chap with an impressive record. The Treble in his first full season was followed by a barren year, as much due to financial constraints as to his mistakes. But he made a number of panic buys after losing Barry Ferguson and Mikel Arteta – Emerson and Egil Ostenstad were never close to Rangers quality.

GREEN AND RED

11 Hoops whose Old Firm games have been curtailed by the referee

1. **Tommy Burns** 13 December 1978, Rangers 3 Celtic 2
2. **Frank McAvennie** 26 October 1986, Rangers 2 Celtic 1
3. **Malky Mackay** 16 March 1997, Celtic 0 Rangers 1
4. **Alan Thompson** 26 November 2000, Rangers 5 Celtic 1
5. **Lubomir Moravcik** 7 February 2001, Celtic 3 Rangers 1
6. **Stephane Mahe** 2 May 1999, Celtic 0 Rangers 3
7. **Johan Mjallby** 21 April 2002, Celtic 1 Rangers 1
8. **John Hartson** 21 April 2002, Celtic 1 Rangers 1
9. **Neil Lennon** 16 March 2003, Celtic 1 Rangers 2
10. **Alan Thompson** 20 November 2004, Rangers 2 Celtic 0
11. **Chris Sutton** 20 November 2004, Rangers 2 Celtic 0

HAPPY HUNTING GROUNDS

11 stadia that have been good for the Gers

1. The Nou Camp
Barcelona's spectacular stadium was home to Rangers' greatest-ever triumph – the 1972 Cup Winners' Cup win over Dynamo Moscow.

2. Tannadice
Dundee United's stadium was the scene of celebrations for the Gers as Brian Laudrup's header in 1997 sealed the record-equalling nine in a row.

3. Elland Road
Scene of one of Rangers' most impressive European performances as the Gers emerged victorious over the English favourites.

4. Hampden
The national stadium has traditionally been kind to the Gers as their haul of 24 League Cups and 31 Scottish Cup triumphs shows.

5. Parkhead
Rangers and Celtic are so closely linked that the Hoops' ground has to feature in this list. There have been plenty of bad days in Glasgow's East End, but some good. The 1999 league title was won there, for one.

6. Pittodrie
Victory at Parkhead is the most satisfying result for Rangers fans, but a win at Pittodrie comes a close second. They clinched the 1987 league title there.

7. Flesher's Haugh
This public park near the Clyde was home for Glasgow Rangers' first games.

8. Artemio Franchi
Two of the Gers' most exciting recent signings were spotted at the Fiorentina stadium. Andrei Kanchelskis and Brian Laudrup both had unsuccessful spells with the Italian outfit before moving to Ibrox.

9. Goodison Park
Home to Everton and, in turn, a huge number of Gers, past and present. Paul Gascoigne, Andy Gray, Duncan Ferguson, Stuart McCall, Paul Rideout, Trevor Steven and Richard Gough are just a handful to have earned their corn at the Merseyside ground and at Ibrox. But Walter Smith came unstuck managing the toffees.

10. Parc des Princes
Scene of the Gers' dramatic UEFA Cup shoot-out win over Paris St Germain in 2001/2002.

11. Philips Stadium
The venue for one of the Gers' most dramatic wins on the road in Europe. Robert Russell scored against PSV Eindhoven with just three minutes to go to send Rangers through into the next round of the European Cup.

HAT-TRICK HEROES
11 Gers strikers who had third helpings

1. Ally McCoist
2. Gordon Durie
3. Erik Bo Andersen
4. Paul Gascoigne
5. Derek Parlane
6. Ralph Brand
7. Robert Fleck
8. Tommy McLean
9. Derek Johnstone
10. Alec Cleland
11. Ian Ferguson

HOLD THE FRONT PAGE

11 scandals involving Gers players

1. Willie Johnston

'Bud' scored 125 goals for the Gers including two in the 1972 Cup Winners' Cup final, but was sent off 20 times in his career and sent home from the 1978 World Cup finals for failing a drugs test when he was a West Bromwich Albion player.

2. Maurice Johnston

Mo scored 52 goals in 99 league appearances for Celtic before moving to Nantes. Unable to settle in France, the striker headed back to Glasgow in 1989. He looked set to sign for a second spell with the Hoops, even being photographed in the club's strip. But at the eleventh hour he signed for Rangers for £1.5m. This was the first time the Gers had knowingly signed a Catholic player and to make matters even more controversial, they'd done it from under the nose of their rivals. The transfer divided the city and made front- and back-page headlines. Indeed, the effects of the move can still be felt today. In March 2005 the striker was lined up to feature in an Old Firm charity match. He was scheduled to play 45 minutes for each side, but a group of Celtic fans began to organise a boycott of the event, furious over what had happened around 16 years before. Johnston was forced to pull out of the event.

3. Chris Woods and Terry Butcher

These two, along with Celtic's Frank McAvennie, were sent off in a volatile Old Firm clash. After the game, the law charged the trio and Graham Roberts with "behaviour likely to cause a breach of the peace". When the verdicts were delivered, McAvennie was found not guilty and Roberts not proven, but Butcher and Woods were both found guilty and fined £250 each. The Rangers pair appealed but lost.

4. Paul Gascoigne

In January 1998, while playing against Celtic at Parkhead, Gazza mimicked playing the flute as if he was in a Protestant marching band. He said he did it to fit in (Ally McCoist is widely thought to have suggested it as a prank), but his actions caused outrage amongst the predominantly Catholic Hoops support and Gazza was heavily criticised in the press.

5. Duncan Ferguson

'Big Dunc' headbutted Raith Rovers' John McStay during Rangers' 4-0 victory in Kirkcaldy, 16 April 1994. The ref didn't send the striker off, but the SFA used TV evidence to ban him for 12 games. The Procurator Fiscal then decided to charge Big Dunc with assault. Ferguson was already on probation after a previous incident and was sentenced to three months in Barlinnie prison. At Newcastle, he was given a convict's suit at a Christmas bash in honour of his time in the Big House.

6. Rod Wallace
The Englishman saw red for the Gers and Stephane Mahe and Vidar Riseth were sent off for the Hoops during the Old Firm game at Parkhead on 2 May 1999. In probably one of the most eventful games in Scottish football history, referee Hugh Dallas was hit by a coin and required five stitches. Rangers finally ran out 3-0 winners.

7. Bob Malcolm
At the end of the 2003/04 season, Malcolm was attending an awards ceremony when he was asked to sign a programme for a fan. The defender/midfielder thought it would be clever to write Bob Malcolm, FTP (crude shorthand for F**k the Pope). He was slammed in the papers. The joke almost ruined his Ibrox career.

8. Paul Gascoigne (again)
Gazza's Rangers career was already turning sour when he was sent-off for kicking Ajax's Winston Bogarde in a Champions League match. The next day, the *Daily Mirror* ran photos of Sheryl Gascoigne's badly beaten face. It almost cost him his England career and went a long way toward ending his spell with Rangers.

9. Donald Findlay QC
Following the Scottish Cup win in 1999, Rangers' vice-chairman was caught on camera celebrating the victory by singing *The Sash*, a sectarian song. The pictures were plastered over the papers and he was later found guilty of professional misconduct. He was forced to resign as vice-chairman and missed out on an honorary degree from St Andrews University because of his actions.

10. Rangers supporters
Meetings between Rangers and Aberdeen are notoriously volatile but the match in January 2002 (Aberdeen 0 Rangers 1) was particularly nasty. Rangers fans pelted the Dons' Robbie Winters with coins as he went to take a corner, leaving him bent double in pain. Furious at the treatment of their player, a group of Aberdeen fans raced along the touchline to confront the visiting fans. Riot police took up position and referee Mike McCurry led the teams off while the situation was calmed down.

11. Andy Goram
'The Goalie' was still making headlines in January 2004. This time the ex-Ibrox keeper was reportedly on the run from gangsters after running up massive gambling debts. It was reported that Goram had been told he was a "dead-man" if he didn't pay up.

IN THEIR WORDS

11 revealing quotes about Paul Gascoigne

1. "He's an intelligent boy who likes to let people think he's stupid. He doesn't have a bad bone in his body, but he does some stupid, ridiculous things."
Ally McCoist 1996.

2. "There's a limit to everyone's patience." **Walter Smith** 1996.

3. "When you crack the same gag five times over it soon wears thin, yet it only makes characters like Gascoigne try harder." Anthropologist **Desmond Morris** 1996.

4. "Even then he was off his head, completely crackers. He would put sweets down his socks, then give them to teachers to eat." **Steve Stone** on his old schoolmate 1995.

5. "I couldn't be like him and he couldn't be like me. I can enjoy a Gazza joke but sometimes I'm glad I'm not married to him because he's talking all the time."
Brian Laudrup 1996.

6. "He's one of the most organised guys I know. He lives things through a Filofax."
Trevor Steven 1997.

7. "He'd have no place in my team. What he gets up to is a disgrace, a disgrace. He's 30 going on six!" **Tommy Docherty** 1997.

8. "The most complete footballer I've ever played with, gifted beyond anyone this country has produced for years and years." Former Middlesbrough team-mate **Gareth Southgate**.

9. "Anything can happen with him. That's for sure." Former Middlesbrough team-mate and Australian goalkeeper **Mark Schwarzer**.

10. "I've made more money out of tears than Ken Dodd." – **Paul Gascoigne**.

11. "A dog of war with the face of a child." Juventus owner **Gianni Agnelli** on Gazza after he had dazzled the world at Italia 90.

JACKS OF ALL TRADES

11 professions adopted by Rangers players

1. Marvin Andrews Worked in a brewery in Trinidad before making it in football.
2. Jim Baxter Began his working life as a miner.
3. Billy Williamson PE teacher with the Royal Navy.
4. Davie Cooper An apprentice printer before agreeing to join Clydebank.
5. Sir Alex Ferguson Was apprenticed as a tool-maker in Govan.
6. Willie Rae Quantity surveyor.
7. Kai Johansen After quitting the game he ran a pub in Glasgow before becoming a players' agent.
8. Ally Scott Went on to sell insurance.
9. Walter Smith Apprentice electrician.
10. Dado Prso Moved to Rouen from his native Croatia but became disillusioned with life in the French lower leagues and actually quit football. He then worked as a mechanic before returning to the game with San Raphael, where he was spotted by Monaco.
11. Willie Waddell After playing and before starting in a turn in management that would see him take over at Ibrox, Waddell worked successfully as a journalist.

KEEPING IT TIGHT

11 particularly mean defensive totals over a season

1. 15 goals in 18 games (1897/98)
2. 16 goals in 34 games (1918/19)
3. 18 goals in 18 games (1898/99)
4. 19 goals in 36 games (1989/90)
5. 22 goals in 38 games (1923/24)
6. 23 goals in 44 games (1986/87); in 36 games (1990/91)
7. 24 goals in 34 games (1917/18); in 42 games (1920/21); in 36 games (1975/76)
8. 25 goals in 18 games (1890/91); in 42 games (1919/20); in 36 games (1995/96)
9. 26 goals in 18 games (1894/95); in 42 games (1921/22); in 30 games (1946/47);
     in 30 games (1949/50); in 36 games (1988/89); in 36 games (1999/2000)
10. 27 goals in 18 games (1892/93); in 38 games (1924/25); in 34 games (1955/56)
11. 28 goals in 26 games (1904/05); in 30 games (1947/48); in 34 games (1962/63)

KIT AND CABOODLE

11 milestones in Rangers strips

1. In 1876/77 the Gers met Vale of Leven in the Scottish Cup. Both sides wore blue, with Rangers adopting a slightly lighter tone than their opponents. This sparked the nickname 'the Light Blues' which is still used today.

2. In 1880 the club ditched all-blue shirts in favour of a striped kit. Four years later it returned to the more recognisable light-blue shirts and white shorts.

3. In 1986 Rangers appointed Freddie Fletcher – yes, that one – as director of sales and marketing to maximise the club's revenue through merchandising and licensing. In this period club shirts carried sponsors' names for the first time.

4. The early 1990s saw Rangers opt for a new away kit. McEwans were the sponsors, but their logo was placed on an unappealing deckchair striped combination of red and Dundee-style dark-blue. Not the best.

5. In the 2000/01 season, Rangers boss Dick Advocaat decided the team's current shorts were too baggy. He felt that they didn't make his team look athletic enough and ordered kit-makers Nike to send a batch of shorter, tighter-fitting shorts. The Dutchman's dabbling in the fashion world didn't go down too well, though. Some of the bigger players felt the new strip constricted their movement whilst 6ft-plus striker Tore Andre Flo was left looking ridiculous. In the end, senior players had to ask the manager to bring back the old shorts.

6. To celebrate Rangers' ever-growing Dutch contingent, the club issued a special orange kit for the 2002/03 season. The move caused some controversy, as it was felt by many that the club was seeking to exploit sectarian attitudes. (Note to the uninitiated: orange is associated with the firmly Protestant Orange Order.)

7. In the 1995/96 season, Rangers sported an interesting quartered red-and-white away shirt, a similar design to that of the blue home shirt worn by the previous season's English champions, Blackburn Rovers.

8. The 2002/03 season saw Rangers take steps to maximise the revenue from kit sales. The club took over the production, marketing and distribution of strips and to cater for the club's ever-expanding fan base, they also added XXXL to their range, alongside special fitted women's shirts.

9. In 2003/04 the club began stocking the kit of their Chinese partners Shenzhen Jianlibao. The agreement meant that the two sides would co-operate in coaching, sports science, player development, exhibition matches and commercial deals. One such commercial deal saw Rangers stock the Asian side's kit. As the Chinese side sport a predominately orange kit, it was again alleged that the Gers were only cashing in on sectarian beliefs held by some of the club's support.

10. The Gers 2003/04 kit was the first to carry the new 'five star' motif above the club badge. The design recognises the club's achievement of becoming the first side to win 50 league titles. A new star will be added for every future 10 titles.

11. In March 2005, Rangers sealed a new deal with manufacturers Umbro which is expected to net the club £6.5m a year.

LANARKSHIRE LADS

11 Gers players from the heartlands

1. **Jim Bett** Hamilton
2. **Davie Cooper** Hamilton
3. **Gordon Dalziel** Motherwell
4. **Tommy McLean** Larkhall
5. **Sandy Clark** Airdrie
6. **Neil Murray** Bellshill
7. **Ally McCoist** Bellshill
8. **Graham Fyfe** Motherwell
9. **John McGregor** Airdrie
10. **Hugh Burns** Lanark
11. **Alex Forsyth** Swinton

LEAGUE CUP HEROES

11 players who've scored in the final

1. **Billy Simpson** Celtic 7 Rangers 1 (19 October 1957)
2. **John Greig** Rangers 4 Airdrie 1 (2 September 1961)
3. **Derek Johnstone** Rangers 1 Celtic 0 (24 October 1970)
4. **Alfie Conn** Rangers 3 Celtic 2 (5 April 1973)
5. **Colin Jackson** Rangers 2 Aberdeen 1 (31 May 1979)
6. **Ally McCoist** Rangers 3 Celtic 0 (25 March 1984)
7. **Ian Durrant** Rangers 2 Celtic 1 (26 October 1986)
8. **Davie Cooper** Rangers 3 Aberdeen 3 (25 October 1987)
9. **Paul Gascoigne** Rangers 4 Hearts 3 (24 November 1996)
10. **Stephane Guivarc'h** Rangers 2 St Johnstone 1 (29 November 1998)
11. **Sotirios Kyrgiakos** Rangers 5 Motherwell 1 (20 March 2005)

11 LIFTING THE CUP

David Haddow
John Drummond
Robert Marshall
Hugh McCreadie
Davy Mitchell
Andrew McCreadie
James Steel
Nicol Smith
John McPherson
John Barker
John Gray

The very first Rangers side to win the Scottish Cup, against Celtic at Hampden Park on 17 February 1894. The Gers won 2-0.

LOCAL LADS MADE GOOD

11 Gers raised in the shadow of the shipyards

1. Ian Durrant
2. Sir Alex Ferguson
3. Jimmy Duncanson
4. Ronnie McKinnon
5. Gary McSwegan
6. Charlie Miller
7. Neil Caldwell
8. Willie Johnston
9. Robert Fleck
10. Robert Russell
11. Tom Forsyth

MADE IN SCOTLAND, FROM GIRDERS

Well, some of them – 11 Ibrox hard men

1. Graeme Souness
One of the first names on any list of the game's hard men. Was sent off on his Rangers debut for booting Hibs' George McCluskey up in the air. He could get away with it – he was the manager, after all.

2. Kevin Muscat
Muscat's reputation as a hard man stems mostly from the days before he came to Ibrox. At Millwall the Aussie was known as a pretty tough cookie. Sent off in his Old Firm debut, he was left out of following encounters with the Hoops because he couldn't be trusted to keep his cool.

3. Terry Hurlock
Another former Millwall player, Hurlock only spent one season at Ibrox but certainly made his presence felt on the pitch and on opponents. The Englishman constantly provoked the wrath of referees and was sent off at Parkhead as the Gers lost 2-0 to Celtic in the Scottish Cup in March 1991.

4. Tom Forsyth
Renowned for his tough tackling: he went into challenges in five-a-side games every bit as hard as he would in normal games. Despite predominantly playing at the back, he also scored the winner in the 1973 Scottish Cup final to give the Gers victory over Celtic, scuffing the ball home from about six inches.

5. John 'Bomber' Brown
Spent nine years with his boyhood heroes, fighting off competition from a number of big-name arrivals to prove a crucial performer for the Gers. Brown was a ferocious tackler with an even more venomous shot, even hitting a hat-trick in a league game in 1985. Brown constantly put his body on the line for the club, never more so than

in a league decider with Aberdeen in 1991. The Light Blues had been ravaged by injuries, but Brown had a series of pain-killing injections to line up at Ibrox. He was never fully fit and collapsed after an hour, but his performance underlined his commitment to Rangers.

6. Graham Roberts
The short but stocky defender arrived at Ibrox from England with a dubious reputation, but he was sent-off only once during his time in Glasgow. He would kick his way through anything to get to the ball but became a crucial player for the Gers, captaining the side to the League Cup in 1988.

7. Harold Davis
The hard-tackling Davis added steel to the Rangers side of the early 1960s. The man from Cupar was an excellent ball-winner but could play a bit, too.

8. Bobby Shearer
A fiery full-back and Rangers fanatic, Shearer had a reputation as a tough tackler. He was committed to the cause and in one match against Hearts in 1960 he replaced injured keeper Billy Ritchie after only eight minutes. Shearer played 82 minutes between the sticks and Rangers somehow won 3-1.

9. Willie Johnston
Bud was a hugely talented winger who picked up bookings almost as easily as he beat defenders. Not perhaps a hard man in the traditional sense, but he was ordered off at least 20 times in his career.

10. Gregor Stevens
Stevens was a quiet, unassuming family man off the field but a fiery character on it. In his five years at the club he was sent off five times and booked on 19 occasions. After being sent off three times in the 1980/81 season, he was handed a six-month ban by the SFA for another dismissal in a friendly against Killie.

11. Gennaro Gattuso
The Italian spent little over a year at Ibrox, but during his short spell with the club he proved himself to be an uncompromising and tenacious midfielder. He moved back home to Salernitana but impressed AC Milan enough to take him to the San Siro. He has become a mainstay there, helping them win the Champions League in 2003.

MARVIN AND THE MAN UPSTAIRS

Marvin Andrews's unshakeable faith has served him well in his time in football, not to mention furnishing sports reporters across Scotland with reams of copy

1. "My dream team is Liverpool, and I know my dreams will come true through God – his timing is perfect."
The big man had better conjure up a Spanish passport if he wants to head to Anfield any time soon.

2. "It wasn't a difficult decision to make – more a matter of time. I prayed to God, seeked his advice, and a few days ago he gave me the answer – to stay. His purpose is for me to still be here at Livingston."

3. "To all intents and purposes, that offer met everything that Marvin was looking for. However at the end of the day, his beliefs would not allow him to come to Tannadice at this stage."
Livy's then assistant coach Allan Preston on how God told Andrews not to move to Dundee United. The man upstairs got this one right – Marvin soon earned a switch to Ibrox instead.

4. "We made an exceptional offer but we can't compete with other forces."
Dundee United boss Ian McCall on his club's effort to land the defender.

5. "Before my career is over I will play in a World Cup for Trinidad & Tobago because I've dreamt and I've prayed about it every day and I know God will answer my prayers."

> BUD WAS A HUGELY TALENTED WINGER BUT PICKED UP BOOKINGS ALMOST AS EASILY AS HE BEAT DEFENDERS

6. "Don't matter who is the coach or who is the manager – I know I am going to play in a World Cup and I give thanks to God."

7. "I pray for success of the club, for the injured player to recover quickly and for wisdom to help the technical staff."
Andrews goes that extra yard to help the team.

8. "It's a different experience from playing in big matches but with God on my side anything is possible."
Marvin becomes a faith healer in his spare time.

11 MADE IN SCOTLAND

Goram

Greig Gough Woodburn Jardine

Souness Baxter

Cooper Brand McCoist Johnston

The Gers have given Scotland some of its finest talent over the years. This line-up is playing a version of 4-2-4, in honour of the great Jim Baxter and the meanest defence in Scottish football history.

9. "I pray in my car, I pray before a game and I pray on the park. So I am in the church." *Marvin explains why he has no objection to playing on the Sabbath: he doesn't have to be in a church to practise his religion.*

10. "I would cause destruction and think wickedness – you name it. I used to fight – I was not a violent person always looking for trouble, but if it came to me I would stand up for myself. I never went all the way and did something really reckless like rob somebody and steal their TV, but I used to take people's fruit off the trees." *Before finding religion Marvin was a different man.*

11. Marvin's heading ability means he's often called on to venture forward at set pieces. On the occasions he hits the back of the net, what do they play over the PA at Ibrox? *I'm A Believer by The Monkees. What else could it be?*

MOVIE, TV, AND MUSIC MOMENTS

Popular culture is saturated with the Gers' influence. If you know where to look...

1. A Shot at Glory
Ally McCoist takes to the big screen with Hollywood star Robert Duvall (worst Scottish accent ever?) in this 2000 story of a lower-league Scottish team under pressure from its American owner. The Gers legend plays a former Hoops star: the archive footage of Ally in his heyday has a Celtic strip imposed over what is obviously a Gers shirt! Ally Maxwell and Claudio Reyna also got in on the act.

2. Hell's Kitchen
The best reality TV series ever – but then the first series was fronted by that well-known former Teddy Bear, Gordon Ramsay, a veritable Graeme Souness of the kitchen, he defines the genre of tycoon known as Doesn't Suffer Fools Gladly.

3. The Planman
Robbie Coltrane starred in this 2003 TV movie, playing a lawyer who seeks to prove you can plan the perfect crime. Set in Glasgow, with cameos from Ronald De Boer, Lorenzo Amoruso, Shota Arveladze, Barry Ferguson, Stephen Hughes, Stefan Klos, Peter Lovenkrands, Charlie Miller, Craig Moore, Kevin Muscat and Steven Thompson.

4. The Book Group
The cult sitcom starred Derek Riddell as a gay football groupie. Riddell was on Berwick Rangers' books when they knocked the Gers out of the Scottish Cup in 1967.

5. Give Us The Ten
This Stock/Aitken single, designed to help the Gers win their 10th title in a row, stalled at No 54 in the UK singles charts. File under: Fate, tempting of...

6. Ae Fond Kiss
Ken Loach's kitchen sink drama begins with a dog urinating on a *Daily Record* billboard which bears the legend: "Church tells Celtic fans no nookie in Seville." In the next scene, a pupil lectures classmates on the subject of religious tolerance. She says: "I am a Glaswegian Pakistani teenage woman of Muslim descent who supports Glasgow Rangers in a Catholic school." For that she is chased through the streets.

7. Mighty Morphin Power Rangers
Not a description which could be applied to the Teddy Bears in the early 1980s. Also provided the butt of many Gers jokes – as in: "You want to see a good Rangers game? Get Mighty Morphin Power Rangers on Game Boy Colour."

8. Blue Heaven
This BBC Scotland documentary series followed youngsters at Rangers' state-of-the-art training facility, Murray Park.

9. Carry On Doctor
The website *www.rangers.openfootball.co.uk* ran a poll asking fans which film best summed up Alex McLeish's stewardship of the Rangers team. This comedy was the most popular choice. Draw your own conclusions.

10. James Bond
007 himself is an occasional visitor to Ibrox. He once memorably advised Gazza that he'd get "a lot of rabbit" at Ibrox.

11. Dougray Scott
If Mr Connery isn't around, Rangers fans could always enlist the help of a man tipped to take over as 007. Alex McLeish – who's a big movie buff – became pals with Hibs fan Scott during his time in management at Easter Road.

MOVING ON
11 Gers who've gone on to manage clubs

1. Willie Waddell
After quitting the game he worked as a journalist before taking over as manager of Kilmarnock and then Rangers.
2. Tommy McLean
Had spells at Morton and Motherwell before joining brother Jim at Dundee United.
3. John Greig
Made 857 appearances for Rangers, winning five championships, six Scottish Cups, four League Cups, then went on to manage the club to more success.
4. Sir Alex Ferguson
The greatest manager Rangers never had.
5. Jimmy Nicholl
Took Raith Rovers into the SPL and to League Cup success in 1995. Now one of the two Jimmys at Aberdeen alongside Mr Calderwood.
6. Sandy Clark
Until May 2005, manager of Rangers – Berwick Rangers, that is. Now coaching assistant to Jimmy Calderwood at Aberdeen.

7. Bobby Williamson
Currently steering Plymouth Argyle off course after spells with Kilmarnock and Hibs.
8. Terry Butcher
The unadulterated misery of his spells with Sunderland and Coventry have been largely forgotten after his fine performance as Motherwell manager.
9. Richard Gough
Just dipping his toe into management with Livingston. Faced a relegation dogfight in his first season.
10. Ray Wilkins
Butch had spells with Fulham and QPR as top dog but has preferred coaching and punditry ("Italians do know how to defend") to managing.
11. Trevor Francis
Sheffield Wednesday, Birmingham City and Crystal Palace have all been lucky enough to enjoy Trevor's distinctive tones.

MR MURRAY

11 landmarks on the road to changing Rangers forever

1. 1988 David Murray buys Rangers from Lawrence Marlborough.
2. 1988 Immediately backs manager Graeme Sounesss' policy of bringing big-name foreign stars to the club. Between them they reverse the talent drain down south, recruiting England internationals like Terry Butcher and Chris Woods.
3. September 1996 Murray announces the club have returned record trading profits of £7m on a turnover of £50m.
4. January 1997 Murray brokers a deal that sees Bahamas-based businessman Joe Lewis invest £40m in Rangers. The deal sees Lewis's company ENIC land a 25.1 per cent stake in the club, at the time the biggest-ever single financial investment in a British football team. After being bought by Murray for just £6.5m back in 1988, Rangers are now valued at £160m.
5. May 1997 Rangers win their ninth consecutive league title.
6. 1998 Appoints Rangers' first foreign coach – Dick Advocaat. During his time with the club the Dutchman attracts a host of top foreign stars, including the De Boer brothers, Giovanni van Bronckhorst and Arthur Numan.
7. 2001 Orchestrates the development of Murray Park, Rangers' state-of-the-art training facility at Auchenhowie.
8. 2002 Stands down as chairman after 14 years, to be replaced by John McClelland. Within a year the club announce debts have risen past the £50m mark.
9. 2004 Returns as executive chairman after the club is heavily criticised by

supporters. Fans are angry at the club's financial situation and frustrated at a lack of investment in the squad.

10. 2004 Masterminds a rights issue to address the club's debts, which sees him invest £50m as the club seeks to reduce the debt, now £72m.

11. 2005 After a trophy-less 2003/04 season, the club has a mixed first half to the new campaign, doing well in the SPL but failing to stay in Europe beyond Christmas. To appease discontented fans, Murray sanctions a string of signings in the January transfer window, including a deal to brings fans' favourite Barry Ferguson back to the club. The midfielder's return happily coincides with the club winning their first match at Parkhead in almost five years.

MY WAY OR THE HIGHWAY

11 chapters in the Graeme Souness guide to man management

1. Graeme Souness was only 16 when he joined Spurs as an apprentice in 1969, but that didn't stop him from soon thinking he should be in the first XI. After a series of 'disagreements' with Souness, Spurs boss Bill Nicholson had had enough and sold the midfielder to Middlesbrough for £30,000 in 1973. Souness' campaign to win his release from Spurs was raised in the House of Commons by MP Tam Dalyell.

2. Wherever he's been, Souness has made waves. In 1989 Maurice Johnston was set to return to Celtic after a spell in France when Souness lured the striker to Rangers. Not only had he stolen a player from under the noses of his club's bitter rivals, he'd also signed the club's first openly Catholic player (at least since World War 2). Rangers were a club with strong Protestant links: such things just didn't happen. Souness took on years of tradition, and revelled in it. Chairman David Murray hinted that if it hadn't been Johnston, it would have been someone else: "Graeme had it in his mind that he had to sign a Catholic." Souness said: "I was always uncomfortable with the Catholic issue because my wife at the time was Catholic and I'd promised to bring up my children as Catholics. I didn't go out to sign a Catholic but Mo was available and the right kind of player. The club's better for it, I think any half-sensible person would agree." He later signed the club's first major black player, Mark Walters.

3. When Souness brought Terry Butcher to Ibrox it was a signal of intent. Here was England's vice-captain, prepared to sign up to the Rangers' cause. The player became a cornerstone of the team through the late 1980s, and many believe it was Butcher's absence through injury that cost the Gers the title in 1987/88. He had helped the Light Blues to three league titles and two League Cups, yet even he couldn't always escape the wrath of Souness. In a game at Tannadice in September 1990, Butcher headed a spectacular own goal and missed a tackle which led to Dundee United scoring again. The Gers lost 2-1 and after the game Butcher was involved in a bust-up with Souness. Two months later, Butcher signed for Coventry City.

4. Liverpool coach Ronnie Moran said of Graeme Souness: "He's so ruthless he makes Kenny Dalglish look like a pussycat." Walter Smith noted: "His mother used to say that wherever he went, trouble would follow quickly." Mum clearly knew best.

5. As a schoolboy Scottish international, he walked out of the squad because another boy had been given the No 4 shirt he coveted. At Spurs, he made just one appearance – as a substitute in a UEFA Cup game. As Alan Mullery came off to be replaced, he saw Souness scowling at him. "About bloody time," growled Souness. "I should have been on ages ago."

6. His Scotland room-mate Gordon Strachan had expected Souness to be neat but he was astonished to discover, when they first shared a room, that his team-mate used to put his underpants on coat hangers and hang them in the wardrobe.

7. "Jack Charlton taught me that sometimes the most important thing is just to win," Souness told *FourFourTwo* magazine in 1996. After losing an away game to Dynamo Kiev in the European Cup, he looked at the rule book and found it was permissible – then – to narrow your pitch as long as it wasn't below certain dimensions. On the Tuesday afternoon, the Kiev players trained on the full-size Ibrox pitch. "On Wednesday night they came out and were shocked to discover that, after 15 paces, they were on the touchline. It wasn't purist stuff, but it was within the rules then."

8. Souness always likes to make an impact and he certainly did that in his first game in charge of Rangers, on 9 August 1986 against Hibs at Easter Road. The new player-manager was sent off for a violent challenge that sparked a mass punch-up between the sides. Nine players were booked during the game, which Hibs won 2-1.

9. Controversy has always surrounded his management of certain players, notably Ally McCoist at Rangers. He denied that the Ibrox dressing room was as volatile as the press suggested. "Ninety-five per cent of the time I'd give someone a big hug after the game but that's not such a good story." But at Rangers and Galatasaray, he was rumoured to have had set-tos with his star striker. In Istanbul, he was quizzed about tales that he had punched a striker but he insisted "I told him to sit down and shut up and gave him a gentle nudge on the shoulder to encourage him."

10. His old Sampdoria team-mate Gianluca Vialli insists that Souey can take a joke. "I used to call him 'You Scottish bastard' and he didn't mind. He likes a joke. He once pushed me in a lake. I was wearing my club blazer, tie and trousers and had just polished my shoes." Souness always said his looks set people's expectations: "God gave me this face, though the plastic surgeon had something to do with it."

11. Souness' autobiography began: "Being successful has always been more important than being popular." Who'd have guessed?

NET BUSTING

Rangers' 11 highest goal-scorers

1. **Ally McCoist** 355
2. **Bob McPhail** 261
3. **Jimmy Smith** 249
4. **Derek Johnstone** 210
5. **Ralph Brand** 206
6. **Willie Thornton** 194
7. **Billy Simpson** 163
8. **Jimmy Millar** 162
9. **Davie Wilson** 157
10. **Jim Forrest** 145
11. **Willie Johnston** 125

NEARLY PERFECT GERS XI

Goram

Greig   Butcher   Gough   Jardine

Baxter

Laudrup   Gascoigne   Cooper

Hateley   McCoist

Managed by Willie Waddell. Nearly perfect because it lacks bite in midfield, it would be wise to have Souness on the bench.

NINE TITLES IN A ROW: THE END V DUNDEE UTD. 1997

Dibble

Cleland   Robertson

Petric   Bjorklund   McLaren

Moore

Miller   Gascoigne

Durie   Laudrup

The team that won the ninth league title in a row against Dundee United at Tannadice on 7 May 1997, winning 1-0.

OH ECK!

11 ups and downs in the managerial career of Alex McLeish

1. December 2001 Appointed Rangers manager after doing well with Hibernian. He'd previously experienced a less successful apprenticeship with Motherwell.

2. February 2002 Wins his first Old Firm game as manager as the Gers move into the League Cup final with a 2-1 win over Celtic.

3. May 2003 Becomes the sixth Rangers manager to guide the club to the Treble.

4. 2003 Financial constraints mean the Gers are forced to shed a number of big stars, including Barry Ferguson and Mikel Arteta.

5. 2003 Lack of funds forces McLeish to gamble on several free transfers and bargain buys. Egil Ostenstad, Nuno Capucho and Paulo Vanoli fail to impress.

6. November 2003 The Gers stumble in Europe again. A 3-0 defeat by his former boss Sir Alex Ferguson's Manchester United is one of four defeats in six group games.

7. May 2004 What a difference a year makes. The Gers finish the season empty-handed.

8. August 2004 The Gers miss out on a place in the Champions League as CSKA Moscow knock them out in the qualifying round.

9. August/September 2004 Buys five new players and brings in one loan signing. Hopes are high amongst the Rangers support but the Gers make an indifferent start to the season, drawing with Aberdeen and Hearts and losing to Celtic in their first five league games.

10. December 2004 The Gers crash out of the UEFA Cup after defeat at home to Auxerre.

11. January 2005 After losing to Celtic in the Scottish Cup, the Gers go 11 games unbeaten, closing to within a point of Celtic and beating Motherwell to bag the League Cup.

OLD FIRM AGONIES

Ouch! 11 of Rangers' biggest Old Firm defeats

1. Celtic 6 Rangers 2 27 August 2000
2. Celtic 6 Rangers 2 10 September 1938
3. Celtic 5 Rangers 1 21 November 1998
4. Celtic 5 Rangers 1 3 January 1966
5. Celtic 4 Rangers 0 1 January 1914
6. Celtic 4 Rangers 0 27 September 1897

7. Celtic 3 Rangers 0 3 January 2004
8. Celtic 3 Rangers 0 24 March 1991
9. Rangers 0 Celtic 3 29 April 2001
10. Celtic 3 Rangers 0 7 May 1995
11. Celtic 3 Rangers 0 2 April 1984

OLD FIRM ECSTASIES

That's more like it! 11 of Rangers' biggest Old Firm victories

1. Rangers 5 Celtic 0 2 September 1893
2. Rangers 5 Celtic 1 26 November 2000
3. Celtic 1 Rangers 5 10 September 1960
4. Rangers 5 Celtic 1 27 August 1988
5. Celtic 0 Rangers 4 6 May 1899
6. Celtic 0 Rangers 4 24 September 1898
7. Celtic 0 Rangers 4 2 January 1948
8. Rangers 4 Celtic 0 1 January 1949
9. Rangers 4 Celtic 0 24 September 1949
10. Rangers 4 Celtic 0 1 January 1963
11. Rangers 4 Celtic 0 26 March 2000

> 3 MAY 2003: McLEISH
> BECOMES THE SIXTH
> RANGERS MANAGER
> TO GUIDE THE CLUB
> TO THE TREBLE

ONE-MATCH WONDERS

11 players whose first game for the Gers was their last

1. Willie Walmsley
Turned out on 19 March 1947 in a 4-1 win over Clyde.
2. Jimmy Frayne
Played one league game, against Dundee on 28 August 1948.
3. John Shaw
Kept a clean sheet as the Light Blues beat Morton 1-0 on 26 October 1946.
4. William Beckett
Played in the 4-0 win over Clyde on 10 March 1951.
5. Johnny Woods
Only opportunity was in the 1-0 win over Queen of the South on 26 March 1955.
6. Ross Menzies
Played in the 1954/55 League Cup quarter-final defeat to Motherwell.

7. Sandy Thomson
The 1957 0-0 draw with Stirling Albion was his solitary appearance.
8. Alan Austin
His only game was an Old Firm clash on 21 September 1957. Rangers lost 2-3.
9. Tom Robertson
A 4-0 League Cup semi-final win against Brechin City on 1 May 1958.
10. Andy McEwan
Played the opening game of the 1958/59 season – a 2-2 draw with Third Lanark
11. Bobby Orr
Say hello, wave goodbye after a 3-2 win over Third Lanark on 27 December 1958.

PARTIES AT PITTODRIE

11 more enjoyable days out with our friends in the north

1. Aberdeen 1 Rangers 1 2 May 1987
It was the last day of the season and Rangers were looking to clinch the title. Terry Butcher scored the Gers only goal before the Dons levelled, but a draw was enough to see them finish top ahead of Celtic. It was the first league title since 1978.

2. Aberdeen 1 Rangers 2 25 September 1982
Diminutive Swede Robert Prytz scored with his head to give the Gers victory, their first at Pittodrie in almost eight years.

3. Aberdeen 1 Rangers 5 Scottish Cup third-round replay, 21 February 1962
After drawing 2-2 in the first match at Ibrox, Rangers made sure in the trip north.

4. Aberdeen 1 Rangers 3 13 April 1935
Victory saw the title head to Ibrox and set the club on its way to securing its first ever back-to-back Double.

5. Aberdeen 1 Rangers 5 30 October 1999
Finn Jonatan Johansson bagged a hat-trick as the Gers ran out comfortable winners.

6. Aberdeen 2 Rangers 4 30 January 1999
The Gers were two goals up inside 11 minutes, but the Dons pulled level. With just six minutes to go, the game looked to be heading for a draw but an Albertz penalty and an injury-time goal from Kanchelskis wrapped up all three points for Rangers.

7. Aberdeen 0 Rangers 3 1 December 1996
Sub Charlie Miller completed the scoring after Robertson and Laudrup had given the Gers a two-goal lead.

8. Aberdeen 0 Rangers 1 7 October 1995
Defender Craig Moore grabbed the only goal of the game to grab all three points.

9. Aberdeen 1 Rangers 2 25 September 1982
This win over the Dons was one of the few highlights of a trophy-less season. The Gers could only manage fourth in the league (18 points behind champions Dundee United) and lost in the League Cup final to Aberdeen.

10. Aberdeen 0 Rangers 5 24 October 1959
This hammering of the Dons at Pittodrie set the tone for the rest of the East Coast outfit's season. They finished the campaign just two places off relegation.

11. Aberdeen 1 Rangers 3 29 October 1949
A trip to Pittodrie is always a potential banana skin for the Gers and this season Hibs were chasing them so closely the result was crucial. Furthermore, the Gers' next game was at Celtic and they couldn't afford to slip up heading into the match at Parkhead. Rangers eventually pipped Hibs to the title by a single point.

> BUTCHER SCORED THE GERS ONLY GOAL. A DRAW WAS ENOUGH TO SEE THEM FINISH TOP, AHEAD OF CELTIC

PAYING THE PRICE

11 matches that cost the Gers

1. Rangers 0 Celtic 0 2 January 1905
Heading into this game, the clubs were neck-and-neck in the race for the title. Tensions were high and a pitch invasion meant the match had to be abandoned. Rangers lost the replay 4-1 a month later. They finished the season level with Celtic but lost the title in a play-off.

2. Hearts 3 Rangers 2 Scottish Cup third round, 25 January 1986
This defeat all but brought a premature end to Rangers' season. The Gers were well off the pace in the league and had already crashed out of the League Cup. This loss at Tynecastle left them with nothing to play for.

3. Celtic 4 Rangers 2 21 May 1979
Rangers were hoping to repeat their Treble success of the previous season but this defeat went a long way to handing their rivals the title. To make matters worse, the Gers took the lead and saw Celtic go down to ten men. Rangers could have killed the match off but sat back, allowing the home side to bag four goals.

4. Rangers 0 Kilmarnock 1 2 May 1998
Killie disappeared back down the M77 with all three points, killing any hopes the Gers had of recording an historic tenth successive league title.

5. Hearts 2 Rangers 1 Scottish Cup final, 16 May 1998
After missing out on ten in a row, things went from bad to worse for the Gers. The result meant they finished trophy-less for the first time since 1986 and Walter Smith couldn't add to his haul of Ibrox silverware in his last game.

6. Dundee United 1 Rangers 0 Scottish Cup final, 21 May 1994
Craig Brewster's scrappy goal from less than six yards was enough to give the Terrors victory and end Rangers' hopes of back-to-back Trebles.

7. Rangers 1 Motherwell 2 22 October 1983
This, the Gers' fifth defeat in nine games, piled pressure on boss John Greig. Supporters stayed on after the game to protest at the club's management and Greig resigned less than a week later.

8. Levski Sofia 2 Rangers 1 Champions League, 29 September 1993
The Gers looked to be going through after Ian Durrant had cancelled out Sirakov's opener for the Bulgarians, but they allowed the home team to put them under pressure. Nikolai Todorov fired in a blistering volley off the underside of the bar to send the Light Blues out of Europe. After the highs of the previous season's European campaign, this was a major blow.

9. Rangers 0 Auxerre 2 UEFA Cup, 15 December, 2004
In the new-look competition, teams were split into eight groups with the top three in each progressing to the next round. The Gers won their opening two games, meaning they needed only a point from their remaining two fixtures to make it

through. After defeat in Holland against AZ Alkmaar, it was vital they didn't slip up when French side Auxerre came to Ibrox in the final group-stage game. But Bonaventure Kalou scored twice to win the game for the visitors and Rangers crashed out. The Gers weren't helped by an uncharacteristically poor performance from Jean-Alain Boumsong. The defender was unsettled by speculation over his future and never really looked comfortable against his former team.

10. Rangers 2 Kilmarnock 3 15 December 1934
Killie's win ended Rangers' astonishing 56-game unbeaten home run, a record that spanned three years.

11. Inter Milan 3 Rangers 0 UEFA Cup, 24 October 1984
The Gers' naive desire to attack the Italians in Milan backfired as the home side soaked up wave after wave of pressure then counterattacked superbly to grab three goals. If Rangers had been more restrained they could have gone through – they won the return leg 3-1 but crashed out on aggregate after this showing.

PLAYERS TO PUNDITS

11 Rangers who've moved behind the microphone

1. Mark Hateley
A regular on Radio Clyde and Setanta TV.
2. Derek Johnstone
A key player for Radio Clyde.
3. Gordon Smith
BBC Scotland's main pundit.
4. Arthur Numan
One of the few foreign players to try their hand at punditry.
5. Walter Smith
A frequent contributor to BBC Scotland but now has his hands full trying to turn Scotland's fortunes around. Understandable really: Berti Vogts never did TV and look at the mess he made of things.
6. Ally McCoist
Ally's TV career is starting to rival his playing one. At one point the irrepressible one was the main expert on ITV's *The Premiership* while captaining a team on the BBC's *Question of Sport*.
7. Andy Goram
Never one to shy away from controversy, 'The Goalie' is now a regular guest on

Real Radio's headline-making *Real Football Phone in*.

8. Sandy Clark
Co-commentator for BBC Scotland.

9. Nigel Spackman
The former Gers midfielder is often seen offering his expert opinion on Sky's many football programmes.

10. Ray Wilkins
Another former Ibrox man who's reached for Sky.

11. Trevor Steven
Another Anglo-Ger to star, in his low-key way, on Sky.

RANGERS IN PARADISE

11 victories at Parkhead

1. Celtic 0 Rangers 1 4 November 1996
Rangers were chasing their ninth successive league championship. Brian Laudrup scored the winner and Andy Goram saved Pierre van Hooijdonk's penalty eight minutes from time to put the Gers three points clear and on their way to the title.

2. Celtic 2 Rangers 4 14 September 1968
Davie White took Rangers across the city knowing the Gers hadn't won at Celtic Park in almost five years. The odds were stacked against the Rangers boss, with Jock Stein's Celtic side at their peak. But despite taking on probably the finest Hoops side in history, the Gers ran out 4-2 winners with Willie Johnston grabbing a brace.

3. Celtic 0 Rangers 3 2 May 1999
The Gers sealed their first league title under Dick Advocaat in front of 7,000 away fans. It was the first time the club had clinched the title on their rival's turf. Neil McCann scored twice and Jorg Albertz added a penalty. The win was also the Gers' 100th league triumph over Celtic.

4. Celtic 0 Rangers 2 20 February 2005
Rab Douglas fumbled Gregory Vignal's long-range effort to put the Gers on the way to their first win at Parkhead in almost five years. Nacho Novo grabbed a second to ensure victory in a match that saw Fernando Ricksen struck by a lighter thrown from the crowd.

5. Celtic 0 Rangers 2 30 September 1995
Paul Gascoigne scored his first Old Firm goal ever as Rangers won their second Old Firm game in the space of 11 days. They'd earlier knocked the Hoops out of the League Cup, 1-0.

6. Celtic 1 Rangers 3 30 October 1994
Mark Hateley scored twice to add to a goal from Brian Laudrup. The win in the East End was suitable revenge after Celtic had won the opening Old Firm game of the season, 2-0 at Ibrox.

7. Celtic 0 Rangers 1 8 March 2000
Rod Wallace, signed on a free from Leeds United, grabbed the only goal at Parkhead. This win preceded a barren spell at Parkhead which lasted almost five years.

8. Celtic 4 Rangers 4 Scottish Cup, 16 February 1957
The Gers were trailing 4-2 in this sixth-round match, but Johnny Hubbard scored from the spot before Max Murray equalised with five minutes to go.

9. Celtic 0 Rangers 1 18 April 1927
The Hoops' decision to parade the Scottish Cup on the pitch prior to kick off backfired. The celebrations motivated the Gers instead and they won 1-0 through a Jimmy Fleming goal.

10. Celtic 1 Rangers 3 League Cup, 25 August 1973
Alex MacDonald, Derek Parlane and Alfie Conn scored the goals in this victory.

11. Celtic 0 Rangers 4 League Cup, 31 August 1956
Sammy Baird scored twice as the Gers ran out comfortable winners.

THE GERS MARKED THEIR 100TH LEAGUE TRIUMPH OVER CELTIC WITH A RESOUNDING 3-0 WIN IN 1999.

READ ALL ABOUT IT

11 Rangers headlines

1. No Grudge with Karate Kid *Sunday Mirror*, 2001
Darren Young on his attitude towards Fernando Ricksen after the Dutchman's reckless tackle almost halved the Aberdeen youngster in a game at Pittodrie.

2. Old Firm pair arrive in Lilliput *The Independent*, 1996
Rangers and Celtic were drawn against Keith and Whitehill Welfare in the Scottish Cup.

3. Why the Long Face, Lionel? *Daily Record*, 2005
Former Ibrox keeper Lionel Charbonnier admits he wishes he'd been born a horse. The Frenchman reckons horses "are the perfect athletes".

4. Fernando's a Calm Buster *Daily Record*, 2004
Ricksen's last-minute penalty sparks chaos at Tynecastle.

5. He Ouzos Class *Sunday Mail*, 2005
Singing the praises of Rangers' Greek defender Sotiris Kyrgiakos.

6. It's Rangers in Paradise *Daily Record*, 1984
After the Gers 3-2 Scottish Cup win over Celtic. McCoist scored the winner in extra time to complete his hat-trick.

7. Greig limps around in Moccasins *Evening Times*, 1972
The Rangers captain adopts novelty footwear in an attempt to shake off a foot injury ahead of the crunch European game with Bayern Munich.

8. If Gers aren't Euro Big Boys by 2001, then I'll be a Failure *Daily Record*, May 1997
Chairman David Murray makes big claims… but forgets them when 2001 arrives.

9. 9 in a Blow *Daily Record*, May 1997
Rangers lose 2-0 to Motherwell at Ibrox as they chase nine in a row.

10. Champs on Cloud Nine *Daily Record*, May 1997
The Gers get the better of their jitters to make history.

11. Super Caley Go Ballistic Celtic Are Atrocious *The Sun*, February 2000
Part-timers Inverness Caledonian Thistle beat Celtic 3-1 at Parkhead. Celtic are out of the Scottish Cup and manager John Barnes is out of a job.

RECORD RECEIPTS

The 11 highest attendances for a Rangers game

1. 143,570 1948 Scottish Cup semi-final (Rangers 1 Hibernian 0)
2. 135,000 1946 Southern League Cup final (Aberdeen 3 Rangers 2)
3. 133,750 1948 Scottish Cup final replay (Rangers 1 Morton 0)
4. 132,870 1969 Scottish Cup final (Rangers 0 Celtic 4)
5. 131,975 1948 Scottish Cup final (Rangers 1 Morton 1)
6. 129,762 1953 Scottish Cup final (Rangers 1 Aberdeen 1)
7. 129,643 1963 Scottish Cup final (Rangers 1 Celtic 1)
8. 127,940 1962 Scottish Cup final (Rangers 2 St Mirren 0)
9. 126,599 1966 Scottish Cup final (Rangers 0 Celtic 0)
10. 125,154 1947 League Cup semi-final (Rangers 3 Hibernian 1)
11. 122,714 1973 Scottish Cup final (Rangers 3 Celtic 2)

RED-FACED BLUES

11 Rangers players sent off in Old Firm games

1. Peter Huistra 22 September 1993 (Rangers 1 Celtic 0)
2. Fernando Ricksen 11 February 2001 (Celtic 1 Rangers 0)
3. Barry Ferguson 27 August 2000 (Celtic 6 Rangers 2)
4. Terry Butcher 17 October 1987 (Rangers 2 Celtic 2)
5. Chris Woods 17 October 1987 (Rangers 2 Celtic 2)
6. Graeme Souness 29 August 1987 (Celtic 1 Rangers 0)
7. Scott Wilson 21 November 1998 (Celtic 5 Rangers 1)
8. Alex Miller 13 December 1978 (Rangers 3 Celtic 2)
9. Lorenzo Amoruso 30 September 2001 (Rangers 0 Celtic 2)
10. Claudio Reyna 7 February 2001 (Celtic 3 Rangers 1)
11. Michael Mols 7 February 2001 (Celtic 3 Rangers 1)

SCORING FOR FUN (1)

Rangers' 11 highest-scoring league campaigns

1. **118** 38 games, 1931/32
2. **116** 38 games, 1933/34
3. **113** 38 games, 1932/33
4. **112** 38 games, 1938/39
5. **110** 38 games, 1935/36
6. **109** 38 games, 1927/28
7. **107** 38 games, 1928/29
8. **106** 42 games, 1919/20
9. **101** 44 games, 1991/92
10. **97** 44 games, 1992/93
11. **96** 38 games, 1930/31
        38 games, 1934/35
        34 games, 1956/57
        36 games, 1999/00

SCORING FOR FUN (2)

11 great goal-scoring feats

1. **Sam English** 44 goals in 32 games, 1931/32
2. **Jimmy Smith** 41 goals in 32 games, 1933/34
3. **Willie Reid** 38 goals in 33 games, 1910/11
4. **Jimmy Smith** 36 goals in 32 games, 1934/35
5. **Alex Venters** 35 goals in 33 games, 1938/39
6. **Ally McCoist** 34 goals in 34 games, 1992/93
7. **Ally McCoist** 34 goals in 38 games, 1991/92

8. Ally McCoist 34 goals in 38 games, 1986/87
9. Marco Negri 33 goals in 29 games, 1997/98
10. Willie Reid 33 goals in 32 games, 1911/12
11. Jimmy Flemming 33 goals in 32 games, 1927/28

SCOTTISH FOOTBALL WRITERS' ASSOCIATION PLAYERS OF THE YEAR

11 Gers greats acknowledged by the press

1. John Greig 1966 and 1976
2. David Smith 1972
3. Sandy Jardine 1975
4. Derek Johnstone 1978
5. Richard Gough 1989
6. Ally McCoist 1992
7. Andy Goram 1993
8. Mark Hateley 1994
9. Brian Laudrup 1995 and 1997
10. Paul Gascoigne 1996
11. Barry Ferguson 2000 and 2003

11 SCOTTISH PROFESSIONAL FOOTBALLERS' ASSOCIATION PLAYERS/YOUNG PLAYER OF THE YEAR

11 Gers players saluted by their peers

1. Derek Johnstone 1977/78 Player of the Year
2. John MacDonald 1979/80 Young Player of the Year
3. Robert Fleck 1986/87 Young Player of the Year
4. Ally McCoist 1991/92 Player of the Year
5. Andy Goram 1992/93 Player of the Year
6. Mark Hateley 1993/94 Player of the Year
7. Brian Laudrup 1994/95 Player of the Year
8. Paul Gascoigne 1995/96 Player of the Year
9. Barry Ferguson 1998/99 Young Player of the Year
10. Lorenzo Amoruso 2001/02 Player of the Year
11. Barry Ferguson 2002/03 Player of the Year

SEASONS IN THE SUN

Rangers' 11 best-ever seasons

1. 1927/28 Rangers won the Double for the first time in their history with a 4-0 win over Celtic.

2. 1929/30 The Gers won every competition they were eligible to enter: the league, Scottish Cup, Glasgow Cup, Glasgow Charity Cup, Second Eleven Cup and Reserve League Cup

3. 1946/47 The Gers won another Double, including victory in the first-ever League Cup final against Aberdeen 4-0.

4. 1948/49 Rangers became the first team to win the league, Scottish Cup and League Cup in one season. The race for the title went down to the wire, with Gers beating Albion Rovers 4-1 as title rivals Dundee lost 4-1 to Falkirk.

5. 1949/50 Rangers beat East Fife in the Scottish Cup final 3-0 and edged out Hibs by a single point to win the title.

6. 1952/53 Double success for Rangers once again but they were made to work for it. The Scottish Cup final went to a replay where they beat Aberdeen 1-0.

7. 1963/64 Yet again the Gers won the Treble.

8. 1971/72 Rangers lifted only one trophy this season but it was a case of quality not quantity. Willie Waddell's side landed the club's only European trophy to date, winning the Cup Winners' Cup with a 3-2 triumph over Dynamo Moscow.

> IN 1930, THE GERS WON EVERY COMPETITION THEY WERE ELIGIBLE TO ENTER – A SEXTUPLE!

9. 1991/92 The Gers bagged the Treble, finishing the league nine points ahead of second-placed Hearts.

10. 1996/97 Rangers equalled Celtic's record of nine consecutive championships. The run of success began under the stewardship of Graeme Souness and was finished by Walter Smith. The Gers also lifted the League Cup to add to the joy.

11. 2002/03 Rangers won their most recent Treble in Alex McLeish's first full season in charge.

SEASONS TO FORGET

For masochists only...

1. 1882/83 The club won only eight out of its 29 matches.

2. 1903/04 Finished third in the league and lost 3-2 to Celtic in the Scottish Cup final.

3. 1907/08 The Gers finished third in the table again as Celtic lifted the title. The Hoops also knocked Rangers out of the Scottish Cup in the third round, 2-1.

4. 1908/09 Rangers could only manage fourth in the table as Celtic were again crowned champions.

5. 1965/66 Celtic won the first of their nine-in-a-row league titles, although the Gers did bag the Scottish Cup.

6. 1966/67 Rangers lost in the final of the Cup Winners' Cup the same year that Celtic became the first British side to lift the European Cup. The Hoops also claimed the league title, the Scottish Cup and the League Cup.

7. 1970/71 The club finished trophy-less but Rangers fans could be forgiven for not caring after the events of January 1971. The Ibrox disaster killed 66 people and cast a shadow over the whole season.

8. 1973/74 Celtic won their ninth successive title. Rangers finished five points off the pace in third spot.

9. 1985/86 Rangers finished the campaign with just 35 points from 36 games. It was the side's lowest post-war total.

10. 2001/02 The Gers enjoyed a Cup double but were way off the pace in the league, finishing a whopping 18 points and 21 goals behind Celtic. It was very disappointing for a side containing players such as Ronald de Boer, Arthur Numan and Barry Ferguson, and which had shown it was capable of beating Celtic.

11. 2003/04 Rangers finished trophy-less, ending the season 17 points and 37 goals behind Celtic in the league.

SING UP
----
11 popular ditties at Ibrox

1. Boys in Royal Blue
(Sung to the theme of *The Star O' Rabbie Burns*)
There is a team down Ibrox way
Who wear the royal blue
They win by night, they win by day
With loyal hearts so true
Their fame is known in foreign lands
Where they have one renown
The Rangers process now demands
A valiant victors' crown

Let Hearts and Celtic rise and fall
They havnae got a clue,
But brightly shines abune them a'
The boys in royal blue

If you would gang the Copland Road
To see the lads in the blue,
You'll always find a welcome there
For lads like me and you
The Rangers fans will chant their hymn
Their battle cry proclaims
Oh Follow follow Rangers on
The cry will be the same

Let Hearts and Celtic rise and fall
They havnae got a clue,
But brightly shines abune them a'
The boys in royal blue

2. Follow, Follow
Though the straits be broad or narrow
It's follow we will, follow we will, follow we will
Though the straits be broad or narrow
It's follow we will
We will follow in the footsteps of our team

Follow, follow, we will follow Rangers,
Anywhere, everywhere we will follow on,
Follow, follow, we will follow Rangers,
If they go to Dublin we will follow on

3. There's Not a Team
O not one, and there never shall be one
Celtic know all about their troubles
We will fight till the day is done
For there's not a team like the Glasgow Rangers
No not one, and there never shall be one

4. The Ballad of Alan Morton
He was a proud young Airdrie lad,
Alan Morton was his name
He played for Glasgow Rangers
The left wing was his game

The Ibrox crowd they loved him so
They crowned him king of all
And every time he scored a goal
They sang "Follow on"

Now Alan played his heart away
In Rangers' royal blue
And then on famous Saturday
In Scotland's darker hue

Young Alan laid the English low
The legend it was born
And every time he scored a goal
We sang him "Follow on"

And so that is the story
My father said to me
He said: "Now son when you're a man
Will you do one thing for me?

Each Saturday down Ibrox way,
Though Alan's dead and gone

Every time the Glasgow Rangers score,
Will you sing them 'Follow on"

5. Every Other Saturday

Every other Saturday's my half-day off
And it's off to the match I go
Happily we wander down the Paisley Road
Me and wee pal Jock
We love to see the lassies with their blue scarves on
We love to hear the boys all roar
But I don't have to tell that the best of all
We love to see the Rangers score

Me oh me oh me oh my, oh how we love to see them try
We love to see the lassies with their blue scarves on
We love to hear the boys all roar
But I don't have to tell you that the best of all
We love to see the Rangers score

We've won the Scottish league about a thousand times
The Glasgow is as simple too
We gave some exhibitions in the Scottish Cup
We gave Wembley wizards too
And when the Rangers win the European Cup
As we've done with one before
We'll gather round at Ibrox park 100,000 strong
And give the boys an Ibrox roar

6. Whenever I'm in Times of Trouble

(to the tune of *Let It Be*)
Whenever I'm in times of trouble
Mother Mary comes to me
Singing Glasgow Celtic 1 Caley 3
Celtic 1 Caley 3
Celtic 1 Caley 3
Glasgow Celtic 1 Caley 3

7. Who's That Team We Call the Rangers?

I have often heard that Real Madrid is the greatest football team
I have even heard that Anderlecht is the best you've ever seen

> **"WHENEVER I'M IN TIMES OF TROUBLE, MOTHER MARY COMES TO ME, SINGING CELTIC 1 CALEY 3"**

There's Manchester United and there's Tottenham Hotspur too
There is Everton, Burnley, Blackburn just to name a famous few

But who's that team we call the Rangers? Who's the team we all adore?
They're the boys in royal blue and they are Scotland's gallant few
And we are out to show the world what we can do
So bring on the Hibs and Hearts and Celtic
Bring on the Spaniards by the score
And we'll hope that every game, we'll immortalise the name
Of the boys that wore the famous royal blue!

8. Sung to the club's dear friends from Aberdeen…

Sheep-shagging bastards!
You're only sheep-shagging bastards!
Sheep-shagging bastards!
You're only sheep-shagging bastards!

9. We've Got Davie, Davie, Davie, Davie Cooper

We've got Davie, Davie, Davie, Davie Cooper
On the wing, on the wing
We've got Davie, Davie, Davie, Davie Cooper
On the wing, on the wing

Davie, oh Davie Cooper!
Oh Davie Cooper on the wing!
Davie, oh Davie Cooper!
Oh Davie Cooper on the wing!

10. The Bouncy

If you cannae do the Bouncy you're a Celt
If you cannae do the Bouncy you're a Celt
If you cannae do the Bouncy, Canny do the Bouncy
Cannae do the Bouncy you're a Celt

[accompanied by bouncing]

Ahhh, bouncy bouncy bouncy bouncy na na na na na
Bouncy bouncy bouncy bouncy na na na na na
Bouncy Bouncy Bouncy Bouncy na na na na na

11. The Famous Glasgow Rangers

As I was walking down the Copland Road
I met a bunch of strangers
And they said to me
Are you going to see
The Famous Glasgow Rangers?

So I took them up to Ibrox Park
Just to see the flags unfold
After that display they had to say
You're the best team in the world

Some people writing songs about
The land that they adore
And some about who fought and won
Their country's greatest wars
Some others still feel quite content
To use another field
But I can write a song about
A famous football team

As I was walking down the Copland Road
I met a bunch of strangers
And they say to me
Are you going to see
The famous Glasgow Rangers?

SLIM JIM
---
11 defining Jim Baxter moments

1. England 2 Scotland 3 15 April 1967

Baxter's most famous moment came when he was wearing blue, but it wasn't the royal blue of Rangers – it was the darker hue of the national team. A year after England had been crowned World Champions with victory over Germany, Baxter inspired Scotland to victory over their old rivals. In front of 98,283 people, Slim Jim was at his impudent best. The cheeky five seconds of keepy-up he managed on the Wembley turf epitomised his performance that day. He was so good that day he's understood to have said: "Are you not ashamed to be on the same pitch as me?" to England's Alan Ball.

2. England 1 Scotland 2 6 April 1963

This performance didn't have the iconic keepy-ups of the 1967 match, but to many it was an even better showing by Baxter against the Auld Enemy. The Rangers star scored both goals to send Scotland to victory. The first came from club team-mate Willie Henderson's cross – stealing the ball off Jimmy Armfield's toe before firing it past Gordon Banks. The second arrived after Henderson was brought down in the box, Baxter coolly dispatching the penalty.

3. Rapid Vienna 0 Rangers 2 European Cup, 8 December 1964

Baxter ran the show, setting up Jim Forrest for the Gers' first goal and pretty much outclassing the Austrians throughout. Baxter's performance was too much to take for one of the home side. After being nutmegged twice in succession, Walter Stocik took revenge, fouling the Rangers star with a tackle so bad it broke his leg.

4. Rangers 9 St Johnstone 1 League Cup, 15 August 1964

Baxter scored twice as the Gers simply overwhelmed the Saints.

5. Rangers 3 Celtic 0 Scottish Cup final replay, 15 May 1963

The Gers recorded a comfortable win in the replay after drawing 1-1 first time round. In truth Scot Symon's side could have put many more past their rivals but the later stages of the game centred more around the genius of Baxter than on scoring. After going two up, Slim Jim started showboating. It began with keepy-uppy on the touchline and moved on to teasing opponents into the tackle only to pull the ball away at the last second. The greatest show of impudence was yet to come though, as Baxter, in front of over 120,000 fans and against his side's biggest rivals, simply sat on the ball. After the game he hid the match ball up his shirt to present it to team-mate Ian McMillan in recognition of his midfield partner's performance.

6. Rangers 2 Celtic 1 League Cup, 13 August 1969

Baxter never really hit his earlier heights during his second spell at Ibrox, but in this game he showed more than just a flash of his former self. At the time, Rangers had become all too familiar with losing to Jock Stein's mighty Celtic side but Baxter's performance was enough to guide them to victory on this occasion. The Hoops went ahead early on through Harry Hood, but Jim prompted the Gers to a win, scoring twice through Orjan Persson and Willie Johnston.

7. Rangers 8 Borussia Moenchengladbach 0 Cup Winners' Cup, 30 November 1960

Baxter inspired the Gers to this emphatic victory with a remarkable performance. After opening the scoring early on, he was involved in each one of the following seven goals, even pressuring one of Gladbach's players into an own goal.

8. Rangers 4 Partick Thistle 1 9 September 1961
Not a game that springs immediately to mind when thinking back over Baxter's career, but one the man himself picked out as one of his best. Things were going so well in the match for Baxter he admitted he actually started to amaze himself.

9. Rangers 2 St Mirren 0 Scottish Cup final, 21 April 1962
Baxter was in sparkling form as he helped the Gers to a cup Double. Ralph Brand and Davie Wilson were on target in front of more than 127,000 spectators.

10. Rangers 7 Ayr United 3 29 April 1961
The Gers clinched the title as Baxter once again pulled the strings at the heart of the Rangers midfield.

11. Monaco 2 Rangers 3 European Cup, 5 September 1961
Baxter scored one of the goals as Rangers secured this impressive win. He was in inspired form on the day, flawlessly linking the Gers midfield and attack.

STUCK IN THE MIDDLE WITH YOU

11 great midfield duos

1. Robert Russell and Jim Bett
Russell had great touch and displayed good vision during his time in the Rangers midfield. Bett was just as talented, comfortable with the ball at either foot.

2. Ian Ferguson and Robert Prytz
Swede Prytz was a small, stocky figure with a powerful shot – he scored 20 goals during his four seasons at Ibrox. He played alongside Ian Ferguson – a hard-running player with an eye for goal – in the 1985 League Cup triumph over Dundee United.

3. Graeme Souness and Derek Ferguson
Although Souness only played 72 games in the Rangers midfield, he was a world-class talent. He was a fearsome tackler and a fine passer of the ball over short and long distances. The talented Derek Ferguson never reached his potential. He did make telling contributions in his early days, but these became increasingly few and far between. Souness eventually sold him to Hearts in 1990.

4. Graeme Souness and Ian Durrant
In addition to his abilities as a midfielder, Durrant could be deployed as an

emergency striker. Indeed, he scored a number of crucial goals after picking up the knock-downs of centre-forwards. Souness could chip in with the occasional goal, although the five he scored in his Rangers career didn't do justice to the quality of his shooting from the edge of the box.

5. Ray Wilkins and Ian Ferguson
Wilkins spent only two years at Ibrox but is fondly remembered by Rangers fans. An intelligent and composed midfielder, he was complemented well by the likes of Ian Ferguson at the centre of the Gers team.

6. Nigel Spackman and Ian Ferguson
Nigel Spackman arrived at Ibrox from England as Ray Wilkins headed back in the opposite direction. Not as incisive a passer as Wilkins, he was a solid ball-winner and his distribution was good.

7. Stuart McCall and Ian Durrant
McCall was a tough-tackling midfielder who added drive to the Rangers midfield. He was instrumental in the club's unbeaten run in the European Cup in 1992, alongside Durrant who played in nine of the ten games.

8. Tugay and Jorg Albertz
Turkish star Tugay had a thunderous shot and vast range of passing. Jorg Albertz was an even greater shot. He could hit the ball at over 80mph. "Gie it the hammer!" was a frequent cry as the German lined up to take a free kick.

9. Barry Ferguson and Giovanni van Bronckhorst
Barry Ferguson is very good in dead-ball situations and adds positive running to the Rangers midfield. Van Bronckhorst added an extra dimension to the Gers midfield with his pace and movement, and the Dutchman was also dangerous at set pieces, when he could curl or blast the ball past opposition defences.

10. Barry Ferguson and Mikel Arteta
The Treble-winning season of 2003 was as much about these two players as any others in the Rangers team. The pair scored 24 goals between them at a time when the Gers didn't have a recognised front pair.

11. Fernando Ricksen and Barry Ferguson
Since Ferguson's return to Ibrox in January 2005, fans have pinned their hopes on this duo spurring the club back to glory days. Things are looking promising so far. The Gers won their first silverware with the duo at their heart in the 2005 League

Cup final. However Ricksen is a full-back rather than an out-and-out midfielder and it remains to be seen whether he can operate there at the highest level.

SUCCESS AWAY FROM IBROX

Bears who've been winners away from Glasgow

1. Sir Alex Ferguson
After bringing success to St Mirren, he guided Aberdeen to three league titles, four Scottish Cups and the Cup Winners' Cup before switching to Old Trafford. His greatest achievement in Manchester has been guiding the Red Devils to the Premiership, FA Cup and European Cup in 1999.

2. Alfie Conn
After a spell in England, Conn returned to Scotland to play for Celtic. He lifted the Scottish Cup with the Hoops in 1977.

3. Jim Bett
After a spell in Belgium in the mid-1980s, Bett returned to Scotland to join Aberdeen. The midfielder went on to win two Scottish Cups and a League Cup.

4. Jimmy Nicholl
After hanging up his boots, the former Ibrox defender became manager of Raith Rovers. He eventually guided the Fife outfit into the Premier Division and to victory in the League Cup in 1995.

5. Rino Gattuso
Since moving to Milan the midfielder has won the Champions League and Italian Cup in 2003.

6. Davie Cooper
After leaving Ibrox, he lifted the Scottish Cup with Motherwell in 1991.

7. Henning Berg
Holder of 100 caps, the Norwegian captain helped Blackburn Rovers win the Premier League in 1995, and picked up two more championship medals (and a Champions League winners' gong) with Manchester United. He then helped Blackburn win the League Cup in 2002 before ending his career at Ibrox. He was also part of the Norway side that famously beat Brazil in the 1998 World Cup finals.

8. Giovanni van Bronckhorst
Won the Premier League and FA Cup with Arsenal. Now a champion with Barcelona.

9. Graeme Souness
After his time at Ibrox, Souness guided Liverpool to the FA Cup in 1992, Galatasaray to the Turkish Cup in 1996 and Blackburn Rovers to promotion to the Premier League in 2001 and the League Cup in 2002.

10. Duncan Ferguson
Part of the Everton team who lifted the FA Cup in 1995.

11. Paul Rideout
Only seven months at Ibrox in 1992, but scored the winner when Everton won the FA Cup in 1995.

SUMMING IT UP

11 quotes on what it means to be at Glasgow Rangers

1. "I only have a drink when we win a trophy. That's why people think I'm an alcoholic." **Ian Ferguson**

2. "I would walk across broken glass for that club." **John Spencer**

3. "A wonderful club when you're winning, a tough club when you're not."
Richard Gough

4. "While I had fallen out with the board of directors I knew that Rangers were the club. I began to believe the old saying that 'once a Ranger, always a Ranger' because there was just something about Ibrox, about the club which makes you proud to be a part of it all." **Jim Baxter** on his return from Sunderland

5. "I'll never leave Ibrox." **Graeme Souness**, six weeks before doing just that.

6. "At Dundee United, the manager Jim McLean had the luxury of time… At Rangers the club cannot stand that kind of patient and persistent policy. Success has to be immediate." **Walter Smith** on the difference between his time as coach at Tannadice, and as boss at Ibrox.

7. "I told them I didn't collect losers' medals and threw it away, I think a couple of kids fought over who would get it." **Graeme Souness** on the 1989 Scottish Cup final.

8. "He's making the biggest mistake of his life." Rangers chairman **David Murray** on Graeme Souness's decision to quit Ibrox for Liverpool.

9. "I have one regret in my career: that I didn't join Rangers a lot sooner." **Ray Wilkins**

10. "Destroyed by Andy Goram." The words then Celtic boss **Tommy Burns** said he wanted on his tombstone after yet another unshakeable Old Firm performance by the Rangers keeper.

11. "If I get another chance, I'll break your leg." **John Greig**'s less than friendly welcome to future Gers' star Davie Cooper when he visited with Clydebank in 1976.

SUPER ALLY

11 McCoist moments to savour

1. 1993 League Cup final
Ally scores the winner against Hibernian with an overhead kick. To make it all the sweeter, the match was at Parkhead, home of rivals Celtic. The striker had not long returned after suffering a broken leg.

2. Season 1991/92
McCoist becomes the first Scottish player to win the Golden Boot after scoring 41 goals. He then went on to repeat the feat the following season, bagging 34 goals in 34 league games.

3. Rangers 3 Aberdeen 2 23 October 1988
McCoist grabs a last-minute goal to give Rangers victory. The strike saw the League Cup head to Ibrox for the third successive season, the first time in the club's history that had happened.

4. Rangers 2 Leeds United 1 Champions League, 21 October 1992
Ally secures victory on the night when he follows up after John Lukic pushes out Dave McPherson's header. It wasn't a classic goal, but it was a classic McCoist moment – in the right place at the right time in a big game.

5. Leeds United 1 Rangers 2 Champions League, 4 November 1992
After taking an early lead at Elland Road, Rangers had to withstand heavy Leeds pressure. After rebuffing attack after attack, the Gers launched a devastating counter of their own which saw Ian Durrant release Mark Hateley down the left. The Englishman crossed for McCoist to score with a diving header, giving the Gers a 2-0 lead on the night and a 4-1 lead on aggregate. Eric Cantona pulled one back for the Yorkshire side but they couldn't stop Rangers.

6. Rangers 3 St Johnstone 1 League Cup semi-final, 22 September 1992
Ally bags a hat-trick to send Rangers to the final where they beat Aberdeen 2-1.

7. Rangers 3 Celtic 2 League Cup final, 25 March 1984
McCoist puts the Gers two up in normal time but Brian McClair's volley and Mark Reid's last-minute penalty send the match into extra time. McCoist wins a penalty and although his spot kick is saved by Packie Bonner he still manages to net the rebound to complete his hat-trick and win the League Cup for Rangers.

8. Celtic 0 Rangers 1 League Cup quarter-final, 19 September 1995
McCoist grabs the only goal to send Rangers through to the semis. He heads home Paul Gascoigne's lob, bagging his 20th Old Firm goal in the process.

9. Rangers 4 Raith Rovers 0 13 January 1996
McCoist scores the final goal to break Bob McPhail's 230 league-goal record.

10. Alania Vladikavkaz 2 Rangers 7 Champions League, 21 August 1996
Another hat-trick as the Gers book their place in the group stage. His goals see him become the club's record European goalscorer, overtaking Ralph Brand's tally of 12.

11. Airdrie 1 Rangers 2 Scottish Cup final, 10 May 1992
Having scored in the semi-final win over Celtic, McCoist bags the winner in the final.

SUPER SWALLY

11 notable Rangers refreshment rooms

1. Stadium Bar 111-119 Copland Road, Ibrox
Two minutes' walk from the stadium and opposite the underground station.

2. The Doctors 4-6 Cornwall Street, Kinning Park
A smallish pub whose wallpaper has a Rangers crest pattern running across it.

3. The Grapes 218 Paisley Road West, Kinning Park
A, shall we say, fiercely pro-Rangers establishment.

4. The District Bar 252 Paisley Road West, Kinning Park
Another Rangers daft public house in the Gorbals.

5. Curly's 14 Raploch Street, Larkhall, South Lanarkshire
A Rangers pub in one of the Gers' biggest strongholds outside Govan.

6. The Cock Tavern East Poultry Avenue, London EC1
Owned by a consortium of Rangers fans. Money goes back into a London
supporters branch to help to pay for match tickets and to subsidise travel
to games.

7. Annie Millers 39 Ropework Lane
A traditional pub in the city centre, close to Argyle Street and Central stations.
Decked out in all manner of Rangers photos and a great place for fans without
a ticket to congregate on match days. There are mixed opinions as to whether it's
open to the non-Rangers minded.

8. The Louden Tavern Duke Street, Dennistoun
Regular haunt of Rangers diehards. To underline the pub's commitment to the
club, they unfurled a 30ft by 30ft banner in the car park to celebrate the
nine-in-a-row triumph.

9. The Crimson Star Bridgeton Cross, Bridgeton
Another fiercely Rangers pub. It shows all the team's games plus videos of former
triumphs between match days.

10. The Clachan Bar 345-347 Paisley Road West, Kinning Park
A fiercely Rangers bar, perhaps a little too partisan for some. One of several
establishments raided in 2005 as part of a crackdown on sectarianism.

11. The Rosevale Tavern Dumbarton Road, Partick
Near the Clyde, across the water from Ibrox. Owned by former Rangers boss Walter
Smith, but sadly there's not much chance of catching him pulling pints – he's a little
too preoccupied with the national side to be restocking the Doritos.

THERE'S ONLY ONE GLASGOW RANGERS...

But here are 11 clubs who've been inspired to adopt the name

1. **Rangers** Chile
2. **Rangers** Nigeria
3. **Berwick Rangers** England
4. **Queen's Park Rangers** England
5. **Manning Rangers** South Africa
6. **Stafford Rangers** England
7. **Cove Rangers** Scotland
8. **Brora Rangers** Scotland
9. **Kilsyth Rangers** Scotland
10. **Kilwinning Rangers** Scotland
11. **Carrick Rangers** Northern Ireland

TOP CLUB SHOP SELLERS

The 11 items of club merchandise most favoured by fans

1. Home shirt
2. Shirt printing – names and number (Novo and Prso are the current top two)
3. Away shirt
4. Charity wristbands
5. Rangers tartan duvet
6. John Greig *Legend* DVD
7. Easter egg
8. Classic 'signature' football
9. Third strip shirt
10. Home shorts
11. Home socks

TOP DEFENDERS

11 rocks on which opposition hopes foundered

1. Eric Caldow

Captained Rangers and Scotland over a 14-year career, picking up a stack of silverware, including five league titles. Technically excellent, Caldow's game was built on his great pace – which he used effectively to frustrate and shepherd opposing wingers.

2. George Young

At 6ft 2in, Young was a towering full-back and part of the club's famous 'Iron Curtain' defence. Although sometimes appearing cumbersome, he was a dominant and effective defender, winning 12 major trophies with the club.

3. Ian McColl

After joining the club from Queens Park, McColl won 13 major honours in 15 years at Ibrox, playing more than 500 games. In the ten-year period he formed part of the 'Iron Curtain', Rangers conceded less than a goal a game. After hanging up his boots, he went on to manage Scotland, where Jim Baxter was to be one of his key players.

4. John Greig

Played a staggering 755 times for the club, scoring 120 goals from the half-back line. He captained the side to their only European triumph in 1972 and won an additional 15 major honours. When on the pitch Greig led by example, encouraging younger players around him and offering help and advice.

5. Colin Jackson

Played for Rangers for almost 20 years, winning three league titles, three Scottish Cups and five League Cups along the way. Unluckily failed a fitness test on the eve of the 1972 Cup Winners' Cup final.

6. Terry Butcher

The centre-half left Ibrox in 1990 after winning three league titles and two League Cups. A fearsome competitor, he was known to take his frustrations out on anything from doors to fire extinguishers during his time as a player and now as a manager.

7. Richard Gough

The Scotland star won a staggering 18 major honours with the Gers and followed on from Terry Butcher as a truly inspirational Rangers captain.

8. Sandy Jardine

Nicknamed Sandy because of his hair colour (his real first name was William), the Edinburgh-born defender won 14 major honours during his time with Rangers. A solid and reliable performer for the club, he didn't miss a single game between 27 April 1972 and 30 August 1975.

9. John Brown

Although born in Stirling, Brown was a diehard Rangers fan who never gave less than 100 per cent for the club. His commitment to the Gers was underlined in the 1992/93 season when he missed only four games in all competitions as the club won the Treble and stayed undefeated in Europe. All in all, Bomber won 12 major honours with the club.

10. Dave McPherson

In his two spells with the club, McPherson won three league championships, one Scottish Cup and four League Cups. He was predominantly a centre-back but he could be deployed as a full-back or in midfield if necessary. The Paisley-born star also brought goals to the Rangers team, hitting the back of the net 32 times during his time at Ibrox.

11. Lorenzo Amoruso

The Italian was guilty of the occasional howler and wayward free kick while at Ibrox, but he also turned in a number of crucial performances at a time when the side was crying out for leadership. The former Fiorentina defender displayed good technique combined with a physical presence that many forwards found difficult to deal with. He was named the Players' Player of the Year in 2001/02.

TOP KEEPERS

11 of Rangers' best shot-stoppers

1. Andy Goram

Goram moved to Ibrox from Hibernian to replace Chris Woods in 1991. He cost the Gers £1m yet more than repaid that investment. Shortly after his arrival he had one or two shaky moments – one of the more notable was a defeat at Tynecastle when he misjudged a long distance effort and let it sail past him, only to see it drop into the goal. However, after a chat with boss Walter Smith about his form he emerged to become arguably the club's greatest-ever keeper. Nicknamed The Goalie, he won five championships with the Light Blues.

2. Stefan Klos

The German arrived at Ibrox in 1998 after winning the European Cup with Borussia Dortmund the previous year. Klos isn't as entertaining off the field as his predecessor Andy Goram, but is equally reliable on it. He has arguably been Rangers' most consistent player since his arrival, and many feel it unfair that his national side has consistently overlooked him. Held in the highest regard at Ibrox, he was named club captain at the start of the 2004/05 season.

3. Chris Woods

The England international joined Rangers from Norwich City in 1986 as Graeme Souness began his Ibrox revolution. Woods was an impressive performer for the Gers and fans were somewhat surprised when he left the club in 1991 to move to Sheffield Wednesday.

4. Annti Niemi

The Finn moved to Ibrox from FC Copenhagen in 1997. Despite his undoubted ability, he never really managed to hold on to the No 1 jersey and moved on to Hearts. He established himself at Tynecastle and since his move to Southampton he's become one of the top keepers in Britain. Has recently been linked with moves to Arsenal and Manchester United.

5. Gerry Neef

The first German to play for the club, Neef was a substitute in the 1972 Cup Winners' Cup win.

6. Peter McCloy

Moved to Ibrox from Motherwell in a player-exchange in 1970. At 6ft 4in the 'Girvan Lighthouse' was a veritable giant in the goal, comfortable with taking crosses and able to get great distance on his kicks.

7. Jim Stewart

Won the Scottish Cup in 1981 and the League Cup the following year. Eventually left the club on a free transfer to join St Mirren.

8. Nicky Walker

A member of the famous shortbread-making family, Nicky was unlucky to find himself playing second fiddle for a large part of his career, first at Rangers to Chris Woods, then latterly to Henry Smith at Hearts. Won the League Cup in 1988 after replacing the suspended Woods. Walker is now back on Speyside, in management at the family firm.

9. Bobby Brown

Part of Rangers' celebrated 'Iron Curtain' defence shortly after the war, Brown was an imposing and athletic figure in the Gers' goal. He won three league titles, three Scottish Cups and three League Cups before moving to Falkirk in 1956. He had the curious habit of always having brand new white laces in his boots for every game; after hanging up those well-maintained boots he eventually went on to manage Scotland between 1967 and 1971.

10. George Niven

The Blairhall-born keeper won five titles in his time with the Gers and proved a reliable performer after replacing Bobby Brown between the sticks. His finest hour came in the 1953 Cup final. After diving bravely at the feet of Aberdeen's Paddy Buckley, Niven went off nursing a head wound. After almost half an hour of treatment he returned, bandaged up, to make a series of top-drawer saves.

11. Ally Maxwell

Understudy to Andy Goram for most of his time at Ibrox, Maxwell nevertheless managed to pick up League Cup and championship winners' medals. He is, however, remembered by many for being at fault for Craig Brewster's winner for Dundee United in the 1994 Scottish Cup final.

TOP MIDFIELDERS

11 of Rangers' best traffic controllers

1. Paul Gascoigne

The Englishman may have his critics, and he may have caused a few headlines for the wrong reasons during his time in Glasgow, but it's impossible to ignore his footballing contribution to Rangers. The Football Writers' Player of the Year in 1996, Gazza lit up the league with his skills during the (just under) three years he spent in Scotland. For each moment of madness there would be ten of sublime ability.

2. Ian Durrant

Govan-born Durrant was hugely successful at Ibrox and always gave 100 per cent, whether in midfield or deployed as a makeshift forward. His career will always be overshadowed by the horror tackle he suffered while playing against Aberdeen in 1988, when the Dons' Neil Simpson shattered his right knee. The injury kept Durrant out of the game for almost three seasons. He did return and continued to play for the club, but never quite hit the same heights. He eventually moved to Kilmarnock and spent almost five years at Rugby Park, first as a player and then as a coach. He returned to join the coaching staff at Ibrox in 2005.

3. Graeme Souness

Although he was nearing the end of his playing days when he came to the club in 1986, Souness was still a world-class talent. After gracing both English and Italian football in notable spells with Liverpool and Sampdoria, he brought a wealth of experience to Ibrox and, most importantly, a winning attitude. He was a ferocious tackler yet could pass the ball as well as any other player to pull on the Light Blue jersey. Prior to his numerous successes in Glasgow he won five league titles, four League Cups and three European Cups on Merseyside.

4. Robert Russell

One of the most skilful players ever to represent the Light Blues, Russell had great touch and vision and helped the team to a mountain of cup success in a decade at Ibrox. During this spell, he won three Scottish Cups and four League Cups to add to the league title in 1978. He is most remembered for a stunning goal scored against PSV in 1978, when he capped a flowing breakaway move from the Gers by curling the ball past the Dutch keeper into the net.

5. Jim Baxter

One of the most skilful footballers to ever play in Britain, let alone for Rangers. His game as a half-back was not about defending – Baxter played football to create and, most of all, to entertain. Whether it was playing keepy-uppy at Wembley to infuriate the English or toying with defenders on Scottish soil, Slim Jim was a showman. His career at Ibrox was spoiled slightly by a series of disputes over money (which actually saw him move to Sunderland and on to Nottingham Forest), but they should not be allowed to detract from his often spell-binding performances in a Rangers shirt.

6. Barry Ferguson

When Ferguson made his debut, coming on against Hearts in 1997, few Rangers fans could have guessed that the young midfielder would go on to become such a crucial player. From that night in Edinburgh he forced his way into the first-team. His performances were such that he was awarded the captaincy at just 24. He was credited by many with single-handedly dragging the team to the Treble in 2003. After that triple success he moved south to Blackburn Rovers to try his hand in the Premiership, but never really settled in England, missing life at Ibrox more than he had imagined. After just 17 months at Ewood Park he won his dream return to Rangers, sealing a last-minute move back to Glasgow during the January 2005 transfer window. Such was his popularity as a player, that scores of supporters trekked out to the club's countryside training complex at midnight on a cold winter's night to celebrate the news.

7. Trevor Steven

The Berwick-born midfielder enjoyed two spells with the club. After joining from Everton in 1989, he left for a brief stint with Marseille in 1991 but returned a year later. During his time in Glasgow, he linked effectively with fellow Englishmen Gary Steven and Nigel Spackman, whether playing on the right of midfield or on the right wing. His second spell with the club was marred by a series of injury problems, but in his first season back he was a crucial player as Rangers won the Treble and came within a whisker of the European Cup final.

8. Stuart McCall

He had the least Scottish-sounding accent, but was a wholly committed player for club and country. McCall was at the heart of the Rangers side that so nearly made it to the Champions League final in 1992/93 and he must be considered one of Walter Smith's shrewdest purchases.

9. Ian Ferguson

Joined the Gers from St Mirren in 1987 after making it very public which club he wanted to play for. Much was expected of the midfielder (who began his career with Clyde) when he arrived at Ibrox. Although he perhaps never quite fulfilled his potential, he was still hugely successful. He won seven league championships, two Scottish Cups and four League Cups to add to the Scottish Cup winner's medal he picked up at Love Street.

10. Jorg Albertz

Arrived at Rangers from Hamburg for £4m in 1996. Although he didn't have the flair of the likes of Russell or Baxter, Albertz was a hugely popular figure with the Ibrox support. He was a solid player and although not blessed with a fantastic turn

FANS TREKKED TO THE CLUB'S TRAINING COMPLEX AT MIDNIGHT TO CELEBRATE BARRY FERGUSON'S RETURN

of pace he did possess a truly thunderous shot. When the German hit a ball, it stayed hit – something that Celtic were frequently reminded of as he scored eight goals against them in his sojourn at Rangers.

11. Giovanni van Bronckhorst

The Dutchman joined the Gers for £5m from Feyenoord in 1998 and instantly

showed great quality on the park. Although more than comfortable at
both left-back or wide on the left, he was most impressive in central midfield. He
had more mobility than the likes of Jorg Albertz but had a similarly ferocious left
foot. He scored 22 goals before moving on first to Arsenal and then to Barcelona.
It is testament to his ability that he was one of few Dutch players to survive a mass
clear-out of his countrymen at the Nou Camp in 2003/04.

TOP SCOTS

11 most-capped Gers players (not all caps won while with Rangers)

1. **Richard Gough** 61
2. **Ally McCoist** 58
3. **Graeme Souness** 54
4. **George Young** 53
5. **Colin Hendry** 51
6. **John Greig** 44
7. **Andy Goram** 43
8. **Eric Caldow** 40
9. **Stuart McCall** 40
10. **Sandy Jardine** 38
11. **Mo Johnston** 38

TRUE BLUES

11 players with the most appearances in a Rangers shirt

1. **John Greig** 755
2. **Sandy Jardine** 674
3. **Ally McCoist** 581
4. **Derek Johnstone** 546
5. **David Cooper** 540
6. **Peter McCloy** 535
7. **Ian McColl** 526
8. **Colin Jackson** 505
9. **Alex MacDonald** 503
10. **Ronnie McKinnon** 473
11. **Tommy McLean** 452

UNFORGETTABLE

11 memorable Old Firm games – not always for the right reasons

1. Celtic 5 Rangers 2 friendly, 28 May 1888
The score might not make pleasant reading for Gers fans, but this was the first-ever meeting between the two clubs. Neilly McNally scored the first goal for the Hoops – interestingly, he had previously played for Rangers. After the game there were no signs of the intense rivalry that was to come. The players went for supper at a nearby hall and toasted each others good health.

2. Rangers 5 Celtic 1 27 August 1988
At the time many fans hailed this as one of the most impressive performances they'd seen from their side. Ally McCoist scored twice to add to goals from Kevin Drinkell, Mark Walters and a fantastic Ray Wilkins volley.

3. Rangers 5 Celtic 0 2 September 1893
The Hoops were reigning league champions when they came to Ibrox with the season only four games old. John Barker became the first Rangers player to bag a hat-trick against Celtic.

4. Rangers 3 Celtic 1 Scottish Cup final, 17 February 1894
This was the first Old Firm Scottish Cup final, and Rangers first ever Scottish Cup. A 20-yard strike from John McPherson was the pick of the goals.

5. Rangers 4 Celtic 0 1 January 1949
The Gers braved the cold to start the year in style, firing four past their rivals. Jimmy Duncanson bagged a hat-trick as the Gers continued their march to Scottish football's first-ever Treble.

6. Celtic 4 Rangers 4 Scottish Cup, 16 February 1957
Four goals were scored in the first 15 minutes at Parkhead – two for each side. The score stayed locked at 2-2 until 15 minutes from the end when Celtic scored twice.

With the Hoops looking certain to win, Rangers were awarded a penalty, which Johnny Hubbard scored to set up a grandstand finish. Max Murray eventually levelled five minutes from time.

7. Rangers 1 Celtic 0 Scottish Cup semi-final replay, 31 March 1992
Rangers' David Robertson was sent off after just six minutes, making Celtic firm favourites to go through. However, Ally McCoist scored just before half-time and the Gers defence held out to record a memorable victory.

8. Rangers 2 Celtic 2 17 October 1987
The Gers went down to nine men after Terry Butcher and Chris Woods were sent off in an incident that also saw Celtic's Frank McAvennie dismissed. Despite being a man down and being forced to put defender Graham Roberts in goal, the Light Blues fought back to salvage a point.

9. Rangers 2 Celtic 0 20 November 2004
Nacho Novo and Dado Prso scored for the Gers, but their contribution only tells a tiny part of this volatile Ibrox clash. Celtic's Alan Thompson was sent off after clashing heads with Peter Lovenkrands. The Hoops player definitely made contact but video replays showed the Dane more than milked the incident. Chris Sutton was then dismissed after picking up a second yellow for an unnecessary handball, leaving the visitors down to nine men. There was talk of a bust-up between the teams in the tunnel at half-time, and police spoke to Rangers' Bob Malcolm about his actions on the touchline. However Celtic boss Martin O'Neill made the biggest headlines. At full time, the Ulsterman rushed on to the pitch to put his arm round midfielder Neil Lennon and proceeded to parade the player in front of supporters. The Hoops manager insisted he was merely showing support to a player routinely targeted for abuse during Old Firm games, but his actions caused some controversy, with many believing he could have incited violence.

10. Rangers 2 Celtic 1 League Cup final, 26 October 1986
Davie Cooper's penalty six minutes from time landed Graeme Souness's first trophy as manager. The first half was largely unspectacular but the game took off after the break. Celtic started brightly, forcing Chris Woods into a spectacular save, before Terry Butcher headed clear from Mo Johnston. After weathering the Celtic storm Ian Durrant fired the Gers ahead, smashing the ball past Pat Bonner. The Hoops then had Frank McAvennie sent off but still managed to score an excellent equaliser through Brian McClair. The game looked to be heading for extra time but Cooper's composure from the spot ensured the Rangers supporters were spared another nerve-wracking 30 minutes.

11. Rangers 1 Celtic 1 2 January 1971

The match should have been remembered for its dramatic conclusion – Jimmy Johnstone put the Hoops ahead with a minute to go before Colin Stein equalised in the final seconds. However, the goals were quickly forgotten as a nightmare unfolded on the terraces. A number of fans making early exits down staircase 13 had turned back after hearing the roars greeting the goals. Some lost their balance in the excitement and confusion, and very quickly this trickle became a wave. Hundreds were swept forward and steel barriers crumpled under their weight. In the end 66 people were killed and more than 140 injured. The tragedy will live on with fans, but at least it did spark the redevelopment of Ibrox into the safe, world-class stadium fans enjoy today.

UP FOR THE CUP

11 Gers who've scored in Cup finals

1. Ralph Brand 15 May 1963 (Rangers 3 Celtic 0)
2. Davie Wilson 25 April 1964 (Rangers 3 Dundee 1)
3. Kai Johansen 27 April 1966 (Rangers 1 Celtic 0)
4. Derek Parlane 5 May 1973 (Rangers 3 Celtic 2)
5. Robert Russell 12 May 1981 (Rangers 4 Dundee United 1)
6. Stuart McCall 25 October 1992 (Rangers 2 Aberdeen 1)
7. Mark Hateley 29 May 1993 (Rangers 2 Aberdeen 1)
8. Gordon Durie 18 May 1996 (Rangers 5 Hearts 1)
9. Ally McCoist 16 May 1998 (Rangers 1 Hearts 2)
10. Rod Wallace 29 May 1999 (Rangers 1 Celtic 0)
11. Giovanni van Bronckhorst 27 May 2000 (Aberdeen 0 Rangers 4)

WE DON'T JUST TAKE FROM GLASGOW, BY THE WAY

11 Bears from Stirling and beyond

1. **Derek Johnstone** Dundee
2. **David Gray** Dundee
3. **Cammy Fraser** Dundee
4. **Davie Dodds** Dundee
5. **Gary Bollan** Dundee
6. **Maurice Ross** Dundee
7. **Stewart Kennedy** Stirling
8. **Duncan Ferguson** Stirling
9. **John Brown** Stirling
10. **Ian Redford** Perth
11. **Steven Pressley** Elgin

WEBSITES FOR BLUENOSES

11 sites for Gers eyes on the internet

1. www.rangers.co.uk
2. www.followfollow.com
3. www.gersfever.co.uk
4. www.bluenosebars.com
5. www.rangersfansvcelticfans.com
6. www.rangersfcsalondonbranch.co.uk
7. www.rangerssupporterstrust.co.uk
8. www.icons.com/ricksen
9. www.narsa.ca (North American Supporters Association)
10. www.broxibears.com
11. www.sporting-life.com/football/scottishpremier/rangers/news

WHAT DO YOU CALL YOUR BEAR?

11 top Ibrox nicknames

1. Jorg Albertz
Nicknamed The Hammer for his ferocious left-foot shot.

2. Alex McLeish
The current Ibrox boss was dubbed Barry by team-mates at Aberdeen after Barry Norman. It may sound strange but the movie-obsessed McLeish would often turn up to training reeling off the critic's descriptions of films.

3. Andy Goram
The Bury-born keeper made the switch to Ibrox in 1991. During his time in Glasgow his performances between the sticks earned him the nickname of The Goalie. At face value it wasn't the most imaginative of titles but was meant to underline the fact that no one could come close to the Rangers number one.

4. Ian Andrews
He wasn't at Ibrox long but shipping five goals in his Old Firm debut helped the keeper earn the unfortunate nickname Julie. So far no one has dared apply the same tag to big Marvin.

5. Willie Johnston
Nicknamed Bud after he turned up for training wearing a long fur coat, similar to the type sported by music hall performer Bud Flanagan.

6. Jock Shaw
Dubbed Tiger for his ferocious tackling style.

7. George Young
Nicknamed Corky because he carried a lucky champagne cork around with him. He was given it by a waiter at the post-match celebrations following the 1948/49 Scottish Cup final win over Clyde.

8. Ally McCoist
Super Ally was his normal tag but when he fell out of favour with Graeme Souness he found himself spending so much time on the bench he was dubbed The Judge. Also known as Dudley after Souness told him he was a "f**king dud".

9. Mark Hateley
Branded Attila due to the fear he struck in opponents.

10. Peter McCloy
The island of Ailsa Craig, in the Firth of Clyde opposite Girvan, has a well-known lighthouse. At 6ft 4in, the Girvan goalie's nickname wasn't long in coming.

11. Tom Forsyth
The centre-half was dubbed Jaws for his tough-tackling style.

WHIPPING BOYS

The 11 sides Rangers most frequently beat in Scottish Cup and League Cup finals

1. Celtic 16
2. Aberdeen 9
3. Hearts 5
4. Kilmarnock 4
5. Dundee United 3
6. Dundee 2
   Morton 2
   Hibs 2
9. Motherwell 1
   Dumbarton 1
   Partick Thistle 1
   St Mirren 1
   Hamilton Accies 1
   Third Lanark 1
   Morton 1
   Clyde 1
   East Fife 1
   Airdrieonians 1
   Raith Rovers 1
   St Johnstone 1

WHO CUT THAT?

11 Ibrox hair-don'ts

1. Peter Huistra
Despite the wealth on offer to modern-day footballers, Peter still seemed content to have his hair cut on the cheap. Best guess is that his style was achieved with a bowl and a pair of scissors.

2. Robert Prytz
The Swede's receding hairline and mullet combination was a sight to behold.

3. Mark Walters
Probably the only player in Rangers history to have a haircut involving right angles. The winger's wedge cut was certainly distinctive.

4. Emerson
If you've seen the Eddie Murphy movie *Coming To America* you'll be familiar with Soul Glow hairspray and its wet-look effects. Emerson to a T.

5. Graeme Souness
The hair may have been slightly less curly by the time Souness made his way to Ibrox, but coupled with the Magnum moustache it still deserves a mention (though possibly not to his face).

6. Terry Hurlock
The defender's shoulder-length black hair may have been fashionable in the early 1990s… then again maybe it wasn't.

7. Mark Hateley
He was renowned for his ability in the air, and no picture of a Hateley header would be quite right without his long hair flowing in the whiplash.

8. Paul Gascoigne
Gazza's time in Glasgow also coincided with a worrying craze for blond rinses. It's a good job people were too busy watching him tie Scotland's defenders in knots to imitate him too much.

9. Colin Hendry
Colin's wife cut his hair – apparently she was a hairdresser. Well, that's what she told him. Rumours were rife around Ibrox that Hendry's career in Glasgow started to go

downhill when he signed up as Pat Butcher's stunt double in *EastEnders*.

10. Lorenzo Amoruso
Ammo played the Italian stallion card well and his greased-up shoulder-length locks were crucial to his success.

11. Ronald Waterreus
The Dutch keeper was born in 1970 and it seems his hair is still trapped there. The poodle perm is pretty bad.

WING WIZARDS
11 Ibrox touchline terrors

1. Willie Waddell
One of the most important figures in the club's history. Waddell occupied positions as manager, general manager, managing director/vice-chairman, director/consultant and honorary director. Before all that, however, he was a fantastic player for the Gers. Strong and quick with tremendous acceleration, Waddell was a great crosser of the ball and a more than competent finisher.

2. Davie Cooper
Coop was so one-footed that Ally McCoist presented him with a fake right leg at his testimonial dinner. Despite being so dependent on his left peg, Cooper was one of Rangers' greatest ever players. His ball control was up there with the very best, and he was deadly from dead-ball situations.

3. Davie Wilson
Wilson combined great speed with good skill and strength to become a crucial player in the 1950s and 1960s. What set him aside from many other wingers was his goal record. He bagged 157 goals for the Gers in 373 games. Indeed he once said: "If I didn't score a goal every two games, I couldn't sleep at night."

4. Willie Henderson
At only 5ft 4in Henderson wasn't the biggest player to grace Ibrox, but his pace was enough to unbalance defenders to give him space to cross. He played a vital role in winning the Scottish Cup in 1962, 1963, 1964 and 1966. A thorn in the opposition's side, Henderson set up the first two goals in the Gers' 3-1 win over Dundee in 1964's classic Scottish Cup final.

11. WAS THIS THE BEST RANGERS SIDE EVER?

Ritchie

Shearer   Provan

Greig   McKinnon   Baxter

Henderson McLean Millar Brand Wilson

Some historians reckon the Rangers side of the early 1960s was, for consistent brilliance, the best line-up they ever had. This is the team which beat Celtic 3-0 in the 1962/63 Scottish Cup final replay.

5. Willie Johnston
Johnston had fantastic pace and possessed great skill, but early in his career he had no desire to play on the wing. Willie was determined to be a striker but got put out wide because of his blistering speed. He scored Rangers second and third goals in the 1972 Cup Winners' Cup win over Dynamo Moscow.

6. Brian Laudrup
The Dane was an instant hero with the Ibrox crowd. After arriving from Fiorentina in 1994, he dazzled fans with his pace and close control. Although he was over 6ft, Laudrup showed grace on the ball and was a crucial player for the Gers, underlined by the fact that he was twice named Player of the Year. He wasn't renowned for his aerial skills, but his header against Dundee United at Tannadice in 1997 sealed the Gers' ninth successive league championship.

7. Tommy McLean
The 5ft 4in McLean was one of the most intelligent players ever to pull on the Light Blue jersey. His strength didn't lie in great speed or dribbling but more on his ability to cross a ball. Tommy would simply knock the ball past the defender and place it onto a sixpence for the likes of Derek Johnstone and Gordon Smith.

8. Mark Walters

Walters – he of the double step-over – made a huge contribution to the club during his two years in Glasgow. Despite playing out wide, he managed 52 goals in 143 games for the Gers. One of his most impressive performances in a Rangers shirt came in the side's 1988 League Cup semi-final with Hearts. Walters scored the opener, set up Scott Nisbet for the second and went on to score the third. His performances become all the more impressive when you take into account the disgraceful racist chanting he often had to endure during his time in Scotland.

9. Neil McCann

After playing in the Hearts side that beat Rangers in the 1998 Scottish Cup final, McCann eventually moved to Ibrox. He had great pace and contributed crucial goals before moving to Southampton for £1.5m in 2003.

10. Andrei Kanchelskis

After falling out with Sir Alex Ferguson at Manchester United, the winger was moved on to Fiorentina. But after a year and a half he arrived at Ibrox for £5.5m in 1998. Kanchelskis had unbelievable pace, which allowed him to beat defenders without the need of a trick or turn, but he had his fair share of skill and flair, too. His most famous piece of bravado in a Rangers strip came in the 1999/2000 season when the Gers beat Ayr 7-0 in the Scottish Cup. He stood on the ball with both feet and raised one hand over his eyes to survey the scene before crossing the ball into the box. Possibly a little patronising towards the underdog opposition who were already getting gubbed, but undoubtedly entertaining for the supporters.

11. Peter Lovenkrands

The Dane doesn't fall into the same bracket as his countryman and fellow winger Laudrup, but he has scored some crucial goals for Rangers, most notably against Celtic. One of his most impressive performances came in the Scottish Cup final of 2002. The Hoops went ahead through a John Hartson header, before Lovenkrands equalised from the edge of the box. Bobo Balde put Celtic ahead again before Barry Ferguson levelled. The game was two minutes into injury time when Lovenkrands turned hero, meeting Neil McCann's cross to win the Cup for the Light Blues.

WINNING WITH A SMILE

11 moments of Rangers humour

1. "Well done, Baldy". The message on the match ball from Rangers keeper Andy Goram to hat-trick hero Gordon Durie after the 1996 Scottish Cup final.

2. "If I'd have scored a hat-trick in a cup final, I'd have been man of the match." Ally McCoist's message to Durie after that game. (Brian Laudrup was man of the match.)

3. Ally McCoist fell out of favour with boss Graeme Souness towards the end of the 1980s and repeatedly found himself on the bench. During one mid-winter match, McCoist emerged at half time with a teapot, teacup and saucer which he set up around him in the dugout. He said it was just to help him keep warm, but it's fair to say his manager wasn't convinced.

4. One day during the early 1980s the Rangers team were training in Glasgow, when for no particular reason Ally McCoist and Cammy Fraser thought it would be a good idea to play a prank on John MacDonald. They grabbed him, stripped him naked and left him tied up in a lift.

5. "I was welcomed to Ibrox by McCoist and Durrant spraying Ralgex all over my underpants." Ian Ferguson.

6. "You can't live in Glasgow and be called Nigel. He's going to be Rab."
Ally McCoist on the arrival of Nigel Spackman.

7. "Gazza said he was taking his wallet out on the pitch with him. I didn't understand what he was talking about until he told me he'd read something in the paper that my mother had said I would either be a footballer or a thief." Marco Negri.

8. "These two boys are not the best of players, but at least they make our team photo a bit more attractive." Ian Durrant on Brian Reid and Derek McInnes.

9. "The Esteemed Mr O'Neill has lost the plot!" Banner unfurled by a group of Rangers supporters at the last Old Firm game of the 2005 season. It followed a sarcastic answerphone message accidentally left on a teenager's mobile by Celtic chairman Brian Quinn: "I'm trying to head off yet another storm created by our esteemed manager who has now, I believe, contradicted the numbers I used in the radio interview given this morning. I'm not going to let him call me a liar!"

10. "Ladies and gentlemen of the jury – oh, that was last week…" Ally McCoist speaking at a supporters function following a recent brush with the law.

11. Police officer: "Do you have a police record, Mr McCoist?"
Ian Durrant: "Aye, Walking On The Moon."

WONDER GOALS

11 top-drawer thrillers

1. Rangers 3 Celtic 1 Drybrough Cup final, 4 August 1979
Davie Cooper juggled the ball over four Celtic defenders before volleying it into the Hoops' goal. It was later voted the greatest-ever Rangers goal by supporters.

2. PSV Eindhoven 2 Rangers 3 European Cup, 1 November 1978
Any winning goal in European football can be considered special, but Robert Russell's strike against PSV had that something extra. With just three minutes left the Gers launched a blistering counter-attack. Russell latched on to an exquisite pass by Tommy McLean before bending the ball round the advancing Dutch keeper. The strike became the BBC's goal of the season.

3. Rangers 1 Celtic 0 League Cup final, 24 October 1970
Not all the best goals are 30-yard thunderbolts. Sometimes the circumstances behind a goal make it great. In 1970, 16-year-old Derek Johnstone made his Old Firm debut in the League Cup final. Despite his tender years he rose to head home the only goal of the game, handing the Gers victory.

4. Rangers 3 Aberdeen 1 28 April 1996
Gazza picked up the ball in his own half and beat two men before storming down the field. Two more Dons were passed as he moved into the Aberdeen area before chipping the advancing keeper.

5. Rangers 2 Celtic 0 26 September 1996
The Gers were going for nine in a row and knew that victories over Celtic would be crucial. After Richard Gough had headed Walter Smith's side in front, Celtic battled hard for an equaliser. John Hughes headed against the Rangers bar, from which the home side launched a devastating counter-attack. Paul Gascoigne ran up with the ball before passing it to Stuart McCall, who moved it out left to Brian Laudrup. He in turn passed it into the path of Jorg Albertz, who was storming down the left.

The German crossed into the box, where the ball was headed home by none other than Gascoigne – the man who had started the move at the other end of the pitch some 30 seconds earlier.

6. Rangers 3 Celtic 1 2 January 1997
When Jorg Albertz arrived from Germany he was nicknamed The Hammer. In January 1997, Celtic found out why. The new Gers star lashed home an unstoppable 30-yard free kick into the visitors' net. TV replays clocked the ball at 80mph.

7. Rangers 2 Celtic 1 Scottish Cup semi-final, 7 April 1996
Ally McCoist had given Rangers the lead but Brian Laudrup's strike stole the show. The Dane played a one-two with Gordon Durie, taking the ball expertly on his chest before racing towards the Celtic goal. Hoops keeper Gordon Marshall came charging out but Laudrup deftly lobbed the ball over him with the outside of his right boot.

8. Leeds United 1 Rangers 2 European Cup, 4 November 1992
Mark Hateley's turn and 20-yard looping volley against the English champions is worthy of inclusion on any list of great goals.

9. Rangers 5 Dundee United 1 23 August 1997
Marco Negri scored all five as the Gers ran out emphatic winners. The Italian would go on to score a remarkable 36 goals that season before losing interest in life in Glasgow and heading home. The striker's third goal saw him expertly juggle the ball before delicately lobbing it over Sieb Dykstra in the United goal.

10. Rangers 5 Hearts 1 Scottish Cup final, 18 May 1996
Gordon Durie bagged a hat-trick but his second goal was something special. Rangers launched a high-speed counter attack that saw Brian Laudrup released down the left. The Dane crossed the ball into the box where Durie volleyed home with the outside of his right foot.

11. Rangers 2 Celtic 1 League Cup semi-final, 5 February 2002
The game had gone into extra time after Bobo Balde had cancelled out Peter Lovenkrands' opener. After 105 minutes of play, up stepped an unlikely match winner – Bert Konterman. He was something of a cult figure at Ibrox but never regarded as a true great or even a great finisher. That didn't stop the Dutchman lashing the ball home past Rab Douglas from 30 yards on this particular evening.

YOU'VE NEVER SEEN THAT BEFORE

11 Rangers firsts

1. 1960/61 Rangers 8 Borussia Moenchengladbach 0
Ralph Brand becomes the first Rangers player to score a hat-trick in Europe.

2. 1960/61 Rangers 0 Fiorentina 2 and Fiorentina 2 Rangers 1
The Gers become the first British side to reach a European Cup final.

3. 1991/92 Ally McCoist becomes the first Scottish player to win the Golden Boot.

4. 1993/94 Mark Hateley named Player of the Year by Scotland's football writers.
He was the first Englishman to receive the award.

5. 26 October 1986 Rangers 2 Celtic 1, League Cup final
Following the Gers' victory over the Hoops, Terry Butcher becomes the first
Englishman to lift the League Cup.

6. September 1983 Dave McPherson becomes the first Teddy Bear to score an away
hat-trick in Europe: grabbing four against Valletta in Maltas in the Cup-Winners' Cup.

7. February 1878 Glasgow Rangers first 'overseas' friendly tour takes them to
Nottingham and Sheffield. In October, they return to Nottingham again and then
play their first friendly in London, beating Clapham Rovers 5-1.

8. 1961/62 Rangers 1 Vorwaerts 0, European Cup
The first Rangers home game in the European Cup to attract less than 1800 fans. The
Berlin Wall having recently gone up, the players in the East German side were refused
entry visas for the UK. The second leg was then played in Malmo and 1781 dedicated
supporters/locals passing by saw Rangers win 4-1 to go through 6-2 on aggregate.

9. 2 September 1893 John Barker was the first Rangers player to score a hat-trick against Celtic. The Gers beat their rivals 5-0 at Ibrox.

10. 1914 Tommy Kelso becomes the first Rangers player to have a surname ending in the letter O. He will be followed by ten others – notably Amoruso and Mikhailichenko – but, as there is no goalkeeper among them, it is sadly impossible to field an entire Rangers XI in formation whose surnames end in O.

11. 17 February 1974 Scottish Cup fourth round, Rangers 0 Dundee 3
This was the first time Rangers had played on a Sunday. Miners' strikes were causing chaos and power shortages. That meant floodlights were banned and games just had to be fitted in wherever they could. It wasn't the best start to playing on the Sabbath, as the Gers lost 3-0. Maybe God was trying to tell them something.

YOU WHAT?

11 competitions the Gers are unlikely to contest again

1. Lord Provost's Belgian Refugee Relief Fund Benefit Match
Clubs often take part in benefit games, but has there ever been one with quite such an uninspired title as this 1916 effort? Rangers beat a Rest of Glasgow side 3-2.

2. Glasgow Cup
The competition died a death as attendances dwindled through lack of interest. Rangers and Celtic are favourites to win most trophies in Scotland but the Glasgow Cup took things to a ridiculous extreme. That said, the Old Firm didn't have things their own way in 1888. Rangers lost the first-ever final to Cambuslang 3-1.

3. European Super Cup 16-24 January 1973
Rangers took on Ajax over two legs, going down 6-3 on aggregate to the Dutch side.

4. British League Cup 17 June 1902, Rangers 2 Celtic 3
The tournament was organised following the first Ibrox disaster of April 1902, with the Old Firm being joined by the top two teams in England. The Gers beat Everton to make it to the final while Celtic overcame Sunderland.

5. The Scottish Emergency War Cup
Following the suspension of organised football in Scotland on the outbreak of World War 2, regional leagues were introduced to cut down on travelling costs

and time. However, it was felt by the SFA that a national cup competition should be retained so they instigated the Emergency War Cup. All League clubs were eligible to participate, but non-league clubs were excluded.

6. The Victory Cup 15 June 1946
Rangers beat Hibs in the final 3-1, but almost had to do without a trophy. In the days leading up to the Hampden showdown, the SFA realised they didn't actually have one for the winners. They sent out a call to Aberdeen to return the Southern League Cup the Dons had won the previous year, so they could award that to the victors. It wasn't the first time that particular trophy had made its way to Ibrox; the Gers had held it for winning the Emergency War Cup and on four occasions for triumphing in the Southern League Cup.

7. St Mungos Cup 14 July 1951, Aberdeen 2 Rangers 1
Every team in Scotland took part in this tournament, which was part of the Festival of Britain. After beating the Gers, Aberdeen made it to the final, losing to Celtic.

8. Glasgow Merchants' Charity Cup
This season-closing competition (once of real significance) ran until 1960 when Rangers beat Partick Thistle 2-0 in the first ever final.

9. IX Trofeo Juan Gamper 21 August 1974
This annual tournament is still hosted by FC Barcelona as a tribute to the founder of the club, with top European and South American teams as guests. There used to be four teams (often including the European champions) taking part but now there are only two.

10. Empire Exhibition Cup 30 May 1938
Staged to mark the Empire Exhibition being held in Bellahouston Park in Glasgow. Eight teams took part in the tournament held at Ibrox – Aberdeen, Celtic, Hearts and Rangers represented Scotland, with Brentford, Chelsea, Everton and champions Sunderland for England. Rangers went down 2-0 to Everton in the first round.

11. The Ibrox International Challenge Trophy 5 August 1994
Rangers were knocked out in the semis by eventual winners Sampdoria. Gers supporters never like to see their side lose but couldn't help but admire the skills of Attilio Lombardo as he turned the Light Blues inside out.